PLANT FUN

Ten Easy Plants to Grow Indoors

by Anita Holmes Soucie

Illustrated by Grambs Miller

FOUR WINDS PRESS ❧ NEW YORK

To my daughter, Juliette, and to Shenli, Pamela, and Forrest

Acknowledgments. I wish to thank Clarence E. Steinbauer, Research Horticulturist (Retired), U.S.D.A., for providing information on the sweet potato and reading and commenting on portions of the manuscript. Also, special thanks to Dorothy Hickey for use of her library; to my editor, Judith R. Whipple, and my agent, Josephine Rogers, for help and encouragement; and to my husband, Gary A. Soucie, for his comments and assistance and for living in a home in which every window sill has become a jungle.

Library of Congress Cataloging in Publication Data
Soucie, Anita Holmes.
Plant fun.
Bibliography: p.
1. House plants. I. Title.
SB419.S57 635.9'65 73-88079

Published by Four Winds Press
A Division of Scholastic Magazines, Inc., New York, N.Y.

Printed in the United States of America
Library of Congress Catalog Card Number: 73-88079
1 2 3 4 5 78 77 76 75 74

Contents

Introduction

Plants make a room feel cozy and natural. To me, they bring something of a spring or summer day into a home.

Have you ever sat in the shade of a big tree in summer? Do you remember the delicious feeling of being wrapped in a world of green leaves and green grass while the sun shone brightly around you? Do you remember the green smells, especially of damp grass?

Most people feel a kinship with plants. We feel at home outside on a thick carpet of green grass or in the shade of a green tree or surrounded by the joyous colors of many blossoms.

When we bring plants into our homes, we usually are trying to capture some of the happiness we feel out-of-doors. Homes, schools, hospitals, offices, and stores can all be brightened with potted plants or cut flowers.

HISTORY OF INDOOR GARDENING

No one knows for sure when people first started raising house plants. But it has been going on for a long time.

Archaeologists have discovered Minoan pots with holes in the bottom. It is believed that these pots were used for raising plants. The Minoans were an ancient people who lived on the island of Crete thousands of years before Christ was born.

And the ancient Greeks, Indians, Chinese, and Egyptians all raised potted plants. The Romans may have been the first to build heated greenhouses. In them they grew flowers all year round.

Modern indoor gardening had an upper-class beginning. Wealthy people of the nineteenth century had plant rooms called conservatories. These rooms were heated and had huge bay windows that let in lots of light. There people grew plants collected from around the globe.

Today indoor gardening is no longer a rich man's hobby only. Even the tiniest pocketbook can afford a potted plant or two. Inexpensive plants from all over the world are available to everyone. They can be bought at dime stores, large drugstores, and supermarkets as well as florists' and nurseries. The central heating of modern homes and apartments makes it possible to raise a number of plants indoors. Conservatories are no longer necessities.

THE SUCCESSFUL GARDENER

Must you have a "green thumb" to garden? There really is no such thing. People are not born with the ability to raise plants. This skill must be learned. It comes with patience, experience, experimenting, reading, and following instructions. If you are truly interested in plants and take the time to learn about them, you will be a successful gardener.

I was introduced to tropical plants and succulents by an elderly friend in Southern California. She had a very beautiful backyard garden. In its center was a rock patio on which she raised potted plants. Each time I visited her, I went home with a new plant and instructions on how to raise it.

I kept my first potted garden on an outside porch. Little by little I began moving plants from my porch to my living room. Trips to nurseries for supplies opened my eyes to the huge range of plants suited for indoor gardening. Soon my apartment was both surrounded by and filled with all sorts of plants—dieffenbachia, begonias, ferns, philodendrons, succulents, and even trees. My interest in plants had grown and so had my green thumb.

When I left Southern California, I left my teacher. It was then that I had to turn to books for help and new knowledge.

USING THIS BOOK

Not everyone has a friend who can teach him how to raise plants. And many gardening books can frustrate a beginner. Directions for raising a particular plant often are skimpy. Most novices need detailed instructions to get them going.

I have written this book with you, the beginner, in mind. It is my hope that you will learn the art of successful indoor gardening easily by following the step-by-step instructions in this book.

The first two chapters give general instructions on how to care for plants. They cover such topics as how to water, how to fertilize, and how to mix soil. Chapter Three deals with plant propagation. Each of the next ten chapters gives directions on how to care for a specific plant. These chapters are followed by ones on making terrariums and on arranging and displaying plants.

The glossary at the end of the book defines most of the gardening terms used in the book. It also describes many of the gardening supplies referred to. Use the glossary whenever you are in doubt about the meaning of a word or term. Terms such as tight pot, crock, propagate, and prune can be found there.

Think of Chapters One through Three, plus the glossary, as your indoor gardening reference. You will refer to the individual plant chapters for instructions on how often to water a particular plant or what type of soil to put it in. Then consult Chapters One and Two for directions on how best to carry out these instructions. Consult Chapter Three for the techniques of propagating plants.

Chapter Sixteen gives information on how to diagnose problems. Consult the chart on page 112 if something seems wrong with a plant.

WHAT PLANTS NEED

Plants grow in partnership with soil, water, sun, and air. Through their roots, plants take in minerals and water from the soil. Through their leaves, they take in carbon dioxide from the air. Using the energy of the sun, green plants turn the carbon dioxide, water, and mineral nutrients into food. They use this food to grow and to reproduce.

All green plants have the same basic requirements. But they need them in different quantities. Some need more water than others. Some need more minerals or more sun.

A potted plant is living with a handicap. It has been robbed of its natural environment. The partnership of air, water, soil, and sun that it is suited for does not exist in your home.

Your potted plant will require a new partner in its environment to keep it healthy—you, the gardener. You must see that it gets what it would if it were living in its natural environment. You must supply it with its rain, its humidity, its nutrient-rich soil, its fresh air, and its light. You also must keep it clean and free of insects, disease, and dead and unwanted growth.

This is a tall order and a big responsibility. But the rewards are great. There is nothing quite so satisfying as having someone say, "My, you must really have a green thumb. Your plants are really doing great."

BUYING AND SELECTING YOUR PLANT

I would suggest that you begin your gardening career with only one or two of the easy-to-grow plants discussed in this book. Before deciding on which one, consider these two questions: Do I have a good spot for it? Am I likely to give it the proper care?

You can refer to the charts on page 27 to help you decide if you have a good place for a specific plant. The second question needs a bit more thought.

Some plant enthusiasts can grow just about any plant. But such people are rare. Most of us do better with some plants than with others. I know that I do.

My hunch is that it depends on the type of person you are. Some people are "mother hens." They like to fuss over their plants and are likely to hover over them constantly. Such people might get frustrated with a collection of cacti which require very little care. For them, African violets may be just the thing.

The "fickle Sallys" of the world, however, might do very well with cacti. These are the people who have an on-again, off-again relationship with their plants. Once a week they may get a real urge to do a little gardening. But the rest of the week they may be too busy with other things.

Read Chapters Four through Thirteen on specific plants. Decide what kind of care the plants need. Then decide whether you can give a particular plant the care that it requires.

Once you have chosen a plant, the next step is finding a healthy one. If you order by catalog, you don't have much control. But if you buy your plant at a store, you will want to find one that is growing vigorously and is disease-free.

Check the plant carefully. Are the leaves green and crisp? Is the soil moist? Does the plant show signs of new growth (buds and new leaves)? Does the plant have a nice shape? These are positive signs. They indicate that the plant is healthy.

Avoid plants with any of the following: drooping, limp, or yellow leaves; bone-dry soil; spindly shape; signs of pests or disease.

You can find inexpensive plants at variety stores, discount stores, supermarkets, and large drugstores. Larger selections of plants are available at florist shops, nurseries, or commercial greenhouses, usually at slightly higher prices.

Many commercial greenhouses ship plants by mail. Generally they require a minimum order of at least $5.00.

I Soil, Pots, Crockery, and Pebbles

A pot, a crock, and some soil—that's about all your plant needs to be comfortable in its indoor environment. A crock is a piece of broken earthenware crockery. The pot and crock are its furniture, the place where it sits. The soil is its kitchen, the source of its food and water.

This chapter explains how to pot your plant and how to prepare its soil.

☙ SOIL

Soil is a combination of tiny bits of rock and humus. Humus is decayed plant and animal matter. It is a crumbly substance composed of bits of rotting leaves, twigs, bark, logs, flowers, soil, animals and their droppings. The leaf mold you come across on a forest floor is a type of humus.

The bits of rock in soil give it its gritty feeling. Humus makes soil feel spongy. Both these textures are necessary to most plants. The grit allows water to filter down through the soil freely. The spongy humus helps hold water in the soil and gives roots something to hold onto. It also creates little pockets of air in the soil and holds the nutrients necessary to the plants.

Most garden soils are not suitable for potted plants. They are too heavy. Most do not have quite enough grit or humus to stand up to the watering they will get in a pot. Constant watering tends to pack garden soils into a hard mass. A packed soil does not have much air and it tends to hold water too long. Soggy soil will drown plants. Potted plants need a soil that drains well and remains just moist enough to allow roots to breathe while taking in nutrients and water.

How do you provide a potted plant with the proper soil? You can mix your own. Or you can buy already prepared potting soils in a package or from a nursery.

Packaged soils can be bought at garden centers and at many supermarkets, hardware stores, and variety stores. They are nutritious and have been sterilized. This means they are free of weed seeds, pests, and disease. Most of them are a bit on the powdery side, however, and they don't have much texture. You can use them if you like. But I prefer mixing soil.

Not all plants have the same soil requirements. In general, desert plants like a sandy soil. Tropical forest plants like a humus-rich soil. And plants from the warm temperate zones like something in between.

Here are some recipes to follow for making potting soils. Directions on which recipes to use for which plants appear in each plant chapter. Consult the glossary for a description of the ingredients.

The recipes are divided into parts. You can use any container you like to measure out one part, depending on how much soil you wish to prepare. For instance, if you want a quart of soil, you could measure your parts out in cups. If you want a larger amount of soil, use a quart-sized or half-gallon container to measure out parts. I would not use anything much bigger than a half-gallon, or your mixture will be difficult to mix.

All-Purpose Potting Soils

Use a packaged all-purpose or standard potting soil. Or buy a mixture prepared by your local nursery. Or mix one of these recipes:

ALL-PURPOSE #1
1 to 2 parts sterilized garden soil
1 part coarse sand, vermiculite, or perlite
1 part humus (leaf mold or moistened peat moss)
Bonemeal (optional)*

ALL-PURPOSE #2 (Adds texture to packaged soil.)
1 part packaged all-purpose soil
2/3 part coarse sand, vermiculite, or perlite
2/3 part humus (leaf mold or moistened peat moss)
Bonemeal (optional)*

High-humus Potting Soils

Use a packaged African violet soil. Or buy a mixture prepared by your local nursery. Or mix one of these recipes:

HIGH-HUMUS #1
1 to 2 parts sterilized garden soil or packaged all-purpose potting soil
2 parts humus (leaf mold or moistened peat moss)
1 part coarse sand, vermiculite, or perlite
Bonemeal (optional)*

HIGH-HUMUS #2 (Adds texture to packaged soil.)
1 part packaged African violet potting soil
1 part humus (leaf mold or moistened peat moss)
1 part coarse sand, vermiculite, or perlite
Bonemeal (optional)*

* Bonemeal is a mild fertilizer. Add one teaspoon per quart of soil if you wish.

Sandy Potting Soils

Use a packaged cactus potting soil. Or buy a mixture prepared by your local nursery. Or mix one of these recipes:

SANDY #1

2 parts sterilized garden soil or packaged all-purpose potting soil
1 ½ parts coarse sand
1 part humus (leaf mold or moistened peat moss)
Bonemeal (optional)*

SANDY #2

1 part sterilized garden soil
1 part humus (leaf mold or moistened peat moss)
1 part coarse sand
1 part broken or crushed crockery or small pebbles (about ⅛ inch in diameter)
Bonemeal (optional)*

SANDY #3 (Adds texture to packaged soil.)

1 part packaged cactus potting soil
1 part coarse sand
1 part humus (leaf mold or moistened peat moss)
Bonemeal (optional)*

These recipes are not scientific formulas. Garden and packaged soils differ. You may wish to alter a recipe according to the basic soil you are working with.

If your garden soil has plenty of grit, you may wish to use less sand. If it is low in humus, you may want to add more humus. Let experience be your guide. Mix a small batch of soil at a time, and see how it drains and holds moisture.

How to moisten peat moss. Dry peat moss repels water. It must be moistened before using. Pour hot water over it. Let it soak a few minutes. Then squeeze it out in your hand and use.

How to sterilize soil. For potting, you will want ingredients that are free of weeds, pests, and disease. Packaged soils come already sterilized. You can sterilize your garden soil by baking it in a slow oven, about 200°F, for two hours.

Moisten the soil before baking and let it cool completely before using. Be warned that baked soil smells pretty bad, so get your mother's permission before you use the kitchen.

How to mix soil. You will want plenty of room to do your soil mixing. It's a messy operation. Spread papers under and around you to protect floors and furniture. Or do the job outside.

You will need something to measure with, to stir with, and to mix in. Stir the ingredients well; be sure to bring up the materials from the bottom.

Store unused soil in plastic bags sealed with twist-ties.

POTS, ETC.

Basically there are two kinds of pots—ones with drainage holes and ones without. An inexperienced gardener should stick to the ones with holes. It is harder to drown a plant in these. Once you have learned something about watering plants, you can try a container with no hole.

Other things to look for in a pot are: size and appearance.

You don't want a pot that is too big or too small. A pot that is too

big will hold water too long. One too small won't hold water long enough. Follow this rule of thumb: Transplant seedlings and cuttings into 3-inch pots—ones that measure three inches across the top. Transplant older plants into pots one size larger than the ones they are in. This should be no more than one inch larger measured across the top.

As to looks, please yourself. There are many containers that will suit the plant. The plant does not care what the container looks like, but you will.

The Old Clay Pot

I don't like to spend a lot of money on pots, so I am always on the lookout for bargains. Many nurseries sell secondhand clay pots. I buy these by the dozen. They are the standard home for house plants. And they come in many sizes from very small to extra large. Drainage saucers can be bought to match the pots.

Nothing sets a plant off like a clay pot. Its earthy color and texture blend naturally with green foliage.

A clay pot has other advantages. If one breaks you can use the broken pieces for drainage. A broken clay pot is a gardener's main source of crockery.

And a clay pot is porous. Air, water, and minerals can pass through its walls. This means the clay pot is equipped with a sort of safety valve. If you overwater or overfertilize a plant, excess water and fertilizer can pass out through the walls as well as the drainage hole. The pot also can "breathe." Air passes through the pot walls as soil dries out, providing oxygen to plant roots.

Other Pots

Plastic pots, styrofoam pots, and glazed pottery pots also are useful. You can use any of these if they suit your fancy. If you use a hard plastic or glazed pottery pot, remember this: Don't overwater and don't overfertilize. They do not have the safety valve that the clay pot does.

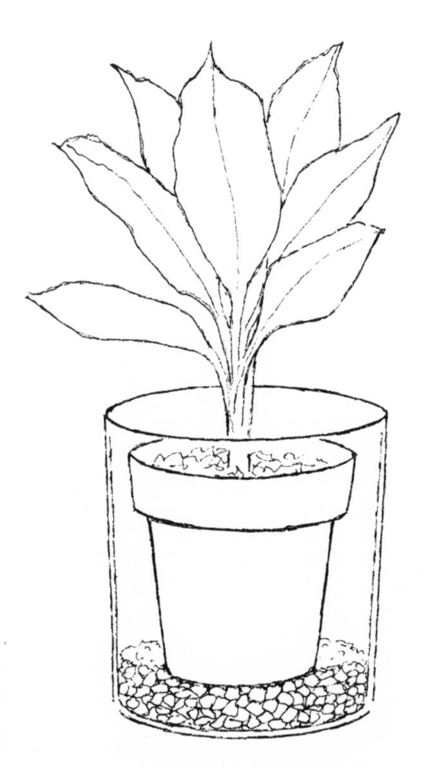

FOR DRESS UP. Perhaps you prefer decorative containers for plants. Many indoor gardeners use cachepots or jardinieres for their potted plants. These are decorated containers or stands in which you set an already potted plant. The jardiniere should be about an inch bigger around than the pot you set inside it. This will allow air to flow freely around the potted plant.

Do this to provide drainage: Place a layer of pebbles at the bottom of the jardiniere. This will keep the potted plant up out of water that drains from pot.

FOR HANGING. Hanging baskets and planters of many descriptions are popular and readily available. To make a hanging basket, you will need a pot which has an interlocking drainage saucer and some string or rope. Take three or four pieces of equal-lengthed rope. Knot together at top and bottom. Connect with another piece of rope which you attach right under the ridge of the pot.

Use heavy-duty eye bolts, screw eyes, or clothes line hooks for hanging a pot from the ceiling. Long hooks, drapery supports, or pot hangers can be used to hang baskets from a wall or windowsill.

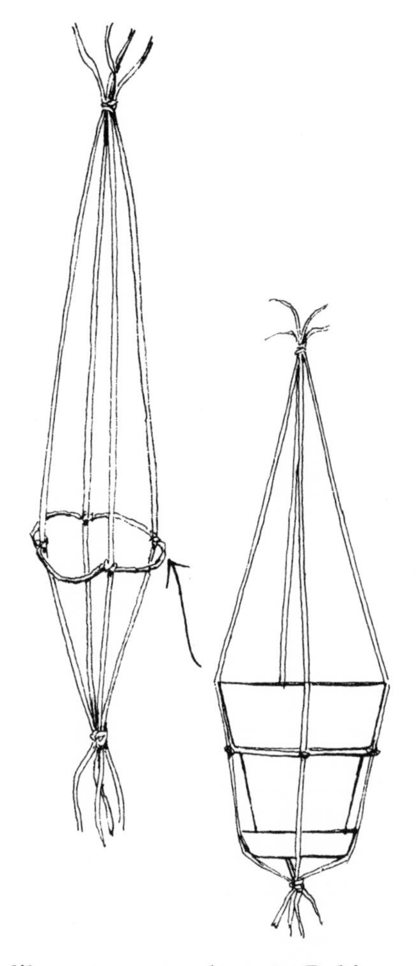

FOR NEXT TO NOTHING. Do you like scavenger hunts? Poking around your house and garage is a good way to find plant containers. Hubcaps, old baking pans, and wooden fruit and vegetable baskets can be used. Line baskets with polyethylene plastic film. The film should be at least twice as thick as plastic kitchen wrap. Plastic bowls, coffee cans, margarine and yogurt containers, styrofoam cups all can be fashioned into containers. Punch holes in the bottom for drainage. Coffee cans and baking pans can be painted in bright colors.

For drainage trays, use aluminum foil pie and tart tins or large jar lids. Or ask your mother for some old saucers.

How to clean your pots. Never put a plant in a dirty container. Scour all containers with hot, soapy water; rinse; and let dry.

To sterilize a pot, soak it for twenty minutes in this solution: 1 part bleach to 10 parts water. Rinse the pot in clear water and let dry.

How to provide drainage. A pot with a hole is already equipped to drain. But you want to be sure the hole doesn't clog up. To do this, cover the hole with a crock. To provide additional drainage, place a layer of pebbles over the crock. Then add soil.

To create drainage in a container without a hole, do this: Place a layer of broken crock at the bottom and cover with a layer of pebbles. Add a few lumps of charcoal to the pebbles to keep the soil "sweet" and free from algae. Algae are tiny, water-loving plants that form a kind of green scum.

POTTING

You've bought your plant; you've got soil and a clean container; now what? You have to get the plant into the new pot without harming it. Here's the procedure:

Provide drainage as discussed above.

Pour or scoop a layer of soil onto the crock or pebbles at the bottom of the pot.

Dampen the soil around your plant.

Remove the plant and soil from the old container. Place your hand around the plant and over the top of the pot. Turn the pot upside down and give it a gentle knock against your hand. If the plant does not come free, knock the edge of the pot gently against a hard surface. (Pry seedlings out of flats with a fork. Try to get all the roots.)

Set the plant in the new pot on top of the layer of soil. Hold it steady with one hand.

Spoon additional soil around the rootball with your other hand. The soil should come to within an inch or so of the top of the pot. Don't set the plant deeper into the soil than it was in its original pot.

Press the soil around your plant very gently to secure the plant in place. Add more soil if necessary to keep the soil at the proper level.

WATER the plant with lukewarm water and set it aside to drain.
CLEAN the plant leaves and wipe the pot clean if necessary.
PLACE the plant on a drainage saucer or tray and display it with pride.

Potting Succulents

Do not water a succulent immediately after potting. Let the plant and soil rest for a day or two to give the plant roots time to heal over before being watered. Then water the plant infrequently for the next few weeks.

REPOTTING

Most plants need repotting from time to time. Some require repotting every year. Others can go for several years in the same soil and pot.

All plants should be repotted when they become pot-bound—the roots have filled the inside of the pot. Roots coming out a drainage hole indicate that a plant is pot-bound. Another sign: A healthy plant ceases to grow and looks droopy.

2 *Tips on Caring for Your Plants*

This chapter gives general information on how to care for house plants. Consult Chapters Four through Thirteen for instructions applying to individual plants.

❧ *PROVIDING THE BEST SPOT*

A plant must have the right environment to grow. Light, temperature, and humidity are all part of a plant's environment. Consider each when selecting a spot for your plant.

Humidity

Humidity is the moisture found in air. Most houses, especially in winter, are dry. They have low humidity. The plants discussed in this book can survive under dry conditions, but most would prefer an environment with higher humidity.

As a general rule, avoid placing a plant over or near a radiator. And if the air around the plant is very dry, take steps to increase humidity. (See page 29 for instructions.)

Temperature

Some house plants are very sensitive to cold. Others are bothered by heat and stuffy air. Fortunately, most house plants do quite well in average house temperatures. If you don't feel too chilly or too warm, the temperature probably is just right for your house plants.

A plant near a window, though, may need protection from window chill on winter nights.

HOW TO GUARD AGAINST WINDOW CHILL. Storm windows provide sufficient protection for your hardiest plants, those that can take minimum temperatures of 50°F. Plugging cracks with window seal also helps.

For more sensitive plants, provide extra protection one of these ways: Place a piece of cardboard, a curtain, or a window shade between the window and the plant at night. Or cover the plant with a newspaper tent.

Light

Some plants require bright light or several hours of full sun a day. Others require shade or filtered light. Some do reasonably well out of the sun altogether.

Adequate light is as important to your plants as water and fertilizer. Without enough light, your plants cannot manufacture the food they need to grow. A few plants can live for long periods in a dim spot. But even these should be moved to a brighter spot occasionally.

The following chart will help you decide how much light your plant will need. The numbers beside the plants indicate the lowest night temperature the plants can take.

Plants for full sun
(At least five hours of sun during winter)

Avocado (60°F)
Cactus (50°F)
Coleus (50°F)
Sweet Potato (60°F)

Plants for partial or filtered sun
(At least two hours of sun during winter)

African Violet (60°F)
Begonia (60°F)
Crassula (50°F)
Dieffenbachia (60°F)
Grape Ivy (60°F)
Philodendron (60°F)
Terrariums (50-60°F)

Plants for dim light

Crassula (50°F)
Dieffenbachia (60°F)
Grape Ivy (60°F)
Philodendron (60°F)
Terrariums (50-60°F)

Many things influence how much light gets into your house. Generally, to get full sun, a plant must be placed in a window which faces south. But not all south-facing windows provide this. A south window shaded by a tree, shrub, or awning may provide only filtered sun.

To judge how much light a spot gets, check it throughout the day. Note at what time the sun's rays shine on the spot and at what time they stop. Remember: The amount of light reaching a certain spot changes throughout the year, depending on the position of the sun.

Use this guide to help you determine where to get the best kind of light for your plant:

Plant needs:	Best place to put plant:
Full Sun	A south or southeast window.
	An east bay window.
	A curved window.
Partial Sun	An east or west window.
	A shaded south window.
	A spot set back from an east, west, or south window.
Dim Light	A north window.
	A shaded east or west window.
	A spot away from a window.

Turn your plants. Plants grow in the direction of their light source To keep your plants growing straight, rotate them. Every day or so, turn your plant about 60 degrees, not quite a quarter turn.

WATERING

Ninety percent of a plant is made up of water. Without water a plant will wilt and eventually shrivel up and die. Water is important to a plant in another way. It carries mineral nutrients from the soil into the plant. So water is of vital importance to a plant.

Proper watering is the key to indoor gardening. It is the single factor that can mean the difference between success and failure. A successful gardener knows when and how much water to give a plant.

A plant can perish when it is not watered. It can just as easily die if watered too often. Soil cannot hold air when it is waterlogged. Without air, plant roots drown and rot. Soil must have a chance to dry out some between waterings.

Watering instructions for individual plants appear in each plant chapter. Some plants do best when soil is always a little moist. Others do best when their soil dries almost completely between waterings. When in doubt, it is better to water your plants too seldom rather than too often.

Here are some watering tips to follow:

☐ Use a finger to tell if soil is damp, soggy, or dry. A light touch or scratch is all that is required. Don't press hard on the soil, or you may pack it down.

☐ Always water plants thoroughly. Overwatering does not come from giving a plant too much water at one time, but from watering too often. Fill the pot with water to the top of the rim. If water runs out the drainage hole, you have watered enough. If not, add more water. Never give a plant a dab of water. While the top soil may appear damp, moisture will not get down to plant roots.

☐ Don't leave a plant standing in water. Once the soil has drained, empty the saucer of all excess water.

☐ If soil dries out to the point where it pulls away from the pot, dampen it a bit. Then water completely. This will keep water from just running out along the sides of the pot.

☐ Water your plants in the morning if possible. Night watering is not recommended. The chances of plant rot increase if plants are watered at times when evaporation is slow.

☐ In general, plants require water more frequently in summer and during periods of growth than in winter resting periods.

☐ Water house plants with lukewarm or room-temperature water. I always keep my watering can full. Then the temperature is right when I want to water.

☐ Some water softeners produce a water that is harmful to plants. If your water softener takes calcium from water and replaces it with sodium, don't use the water from your tap. Get it from an outside faucet instead.

☐ When you have several potted plants displayed together in a group, treat each plant individually. Plants in small or tight pots will require more frequent watering than plants in large, roomy pots. Plants in plastic pots will need less frequent watering than plants in clay pots. Thin-leaved plants, such as coleus, will require water more frequently than plants with thick waxy leaves.

☐ Seeds and seedlings should be bottom watered. Place the container in a bowl or basin. Fill the bowl with lukewarm water to a depth of the plant's soil level. Watering is completed when water is visible on top of the soil surface.

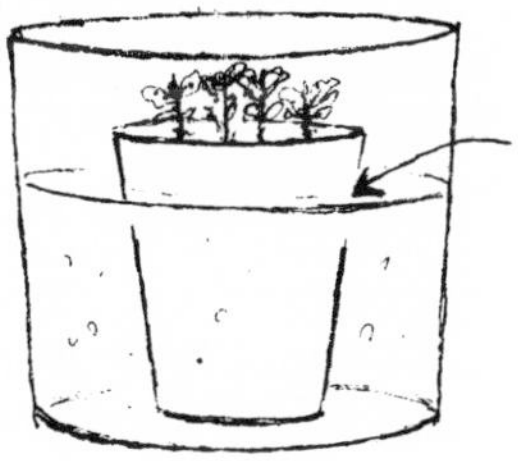

MISTING AND HUMIDIFYING

Most houses are as dry as deserts in winter. Heaters dry out the air. Unless you have a humidifier, you may wish to provide your plants with extra humidity.

Misting

Misting plants with water daily is one way to increase humidity. Use any kind of mister or atomizer that gives off a fine spray. Buy one at

a plant center. Or use an old Windex sprayer or mouthwash atomizer. Wash an old mister before using it on your plants.

Mist plants from a distance of a foot or so with lukewarm water. Moisten only the air and leaves; you don't want to leave large beads of water on the plant. Be particularly careful about this when misting African violets.

Pebble Trays

Pebble trays provide plants with moisture. These trays should be at least 1½ inches deep. Buy them at garden centers. Or use an old cake pan, kitty litter tray, and the like—anything that will hold water and is big enough to extend beyond the reach of your plant's leaves.

Fill the tray with pebbles, coarse sand, or gravel. Set your plant or plants on the tray. Then fill the tray with water up to the top of the

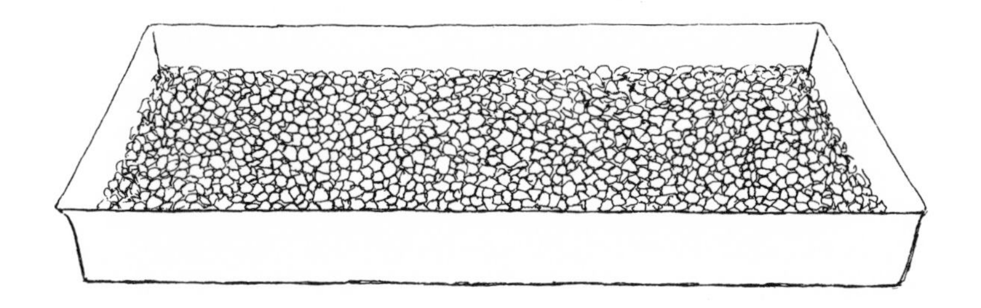

pebbles. Add water as it evaporates. Don't let the water level come up over the base of your pots. The evaporating water will keep the air around your plants moist.

Radiator Buffers

If you must set plants over a radiator, provide a buffer between the plants and the top of the radiator. You can make a shelf over the radiator using blocks and a plank. Or you can put a piece of insulation over the radiator top. Then place pebble trays on top of the buffer.

Grouping Plants

Plants moisturize the air as they transpire water vapor out of their leaves. Group your plants together in one spot or on a pebble tray. They will provide humidity for each other just as the plants in a forest do.

☙ *CLEANING*

A dirty plant is not a healthy plant. Dirt and dust invite disease and pests. They also clog plant pores. Plants are like people. They require showers and occasional tub baths. Always use lukewarm water.

Baths

Sometimes you may want to give your plants a soapy bath. A bath is useful in freeing plants of insect pests and in removing gritty soot.

Turn the plant upside down and swish it gently in soapy water. Be sure to cover the pot and soil with something and hold your hand securely over the top of the pot so that plant and soil won't fall out. Rinse by swishing the plant in fresh water or spray it with a hose.

Showers

Shower most house plants about once a month or when they look dusty or dirty. Use a rinsing hose, if possible, or a sprinkling can. Hold the plant over a sink or tub at an angle and spray with a fairly strong spray. Set the plant out of direct sun to dry.

HOW TO PREPARE YOUR PLANT FOR BATH OR SHOWER. Wrap the entire pot in aluminum foil, a plastic sheet, or newspaper. Hold the wrapping in place around the base of plant when you tip pot.

Sponge Baths

Large plants should be sponge bathed and rinsed. The danger of dropping the plant out of the pot is greater with a large, heavy potted plant.

☙ *FEEDING YOUR PLANTS*

Plants use the minerals found in good soil to make their food. Because the frequent waterings we give our house plants wash out many of these minerals before a plant can use them, potted plants need frequent feedings to keep the soil nutritious and the plant healthy.

There are many types of fertilizer on the market. I prefer those that you dissolve in water. They come in powdered and liquid form. You add a teaspoon or so to the water in your watering can and pour over your soil.

Follow the manufacturer's directions carefully. Never add more fertilizer than is suggested. And do not fertilize more frequently than directed. It is better to fertilize too little than to feed a plant too much. Most house plants do well on a once-a-month or twice-a-month feeding schedule.

Here are a few tips:

☐ Plants in plastic pots require less fertilizer than plants in clay pots.

☐ Plants placed in dim light require less fertilizer than plants in bright light.

☐ A plant that is dormant should not be fed.

☐ Keep fertilizers out of the reach of small children.

☐ Green scum on the sides of pots and white-crusted soil are signs that you are feeding your plants too much.

PINCHING AND PRUNING

Picture this: A healthy plant with crisp green leaves grows up and up and up and then begins to bend. It looks unsightly and uncared for.

What has happened? The plant was not pruned (cut back and shaped). Left to grow in its own way, it got too tall to support itself, and it began to droop.

Many house plants need pruning to keep them bushy and attractive. The idea is to make a plant branch out so that it looks full. Branching in a flowering plant means more blossoms as well.

Starting a plant off right is important. Then, all that is required is a mild sort of pruning called pinching.

Pinching

Coleus, grape ivy, heart-leafed philodendron, crassula, and begonia can be shaped by pinching. Pinching means to remove the budding leaf or growing end of a stem. Use the fingernails of your thumb and index finger or a scissors. Pinching should begin when a plant has developed from four to six leaves. Continue pinching back the plant throughout the plant's life to shape it and keep it bushy or full.

Pinching will halt the growth of the stem and force it to produce branches. The coleus and crassula have opposing leaves—two leaves opposite each other on a stem. It is easy to decide where to pinch such plants. You just take off the newest developing leaves between two more mature ones. The plant will form two new stems at the end.

Plants with alternating leaves such as the begonia are a bit more tricky. You pinch off the little nub or bud that is forming across the stem from the last leaf. Branching may begin lower down on the pinched stem or even at the base of the plant.

Cutting Back

If a plant gets unruly and out of hand, more drastic pruning may be necessary. You can cut several inches off a plant if you need to. Branching will result. Cuts should be made with a sharp knife or razor blade right above a joint—where a leaf joins a stem. Save the severed pieces to propagate new plants.

Non-Branching Plants

Not all plants can be pruned as above. Dieffenbachia, African violets, and many desert cacti do not branch. And they do not get pruned off the top under ordinary circumstances. Consult individual plant chapters for instructions on proper pruning methods.

Keeping Plants Tidy

All plants should be pruned of dead leaves and blossoms regularly. As blossoms and leaves turn brown, pinch them or pull them off as close to a stem as possible. Removing old blossoms encourages a plant to produce new ones.

☙ *TRAINING VINES*

You can train a vine to grow up or around just about anything. To train in this instance means to make a plant grow in the direction you want it to.

Philodendrons are usually provided with a support made of a piece of wood with rough bark. The philodendron has small aerial roots on its stems. These cling to rough surfaces. You merely need to aim the plant in the right direction, and its roots will cling to the bark. Stakes upon which sphagnum moss has been wrapped and tied also will work. The plant is usually trained to wind up and around these. You can assist it by tying it at first.

Sweet potato vines and grape ivy are often trained around windows or trellises. I like to use string to provide support around a window. Attach pieces of string between nails. Use twist-ties to start the plant growing up the string.

If you want a bushier vine, don't hesitate to pinch it out. But don't pinch out your main and longest stem.

CONTROLLING PESTS

Mealy bugs, red spider mites, white flies, aphids, and scale. These are pesky insects that sometimes attack house plants by sucking their juices. A plant covered by these pests isn't going to do very well.

Chances are you will never run across these pests. But just in case, here are some steps to take:

☐ Examine all plants for pests before bringing them home.

☐ Once home, keep new plants separate from others until you are sure that they are free of pests.

☐ Keep plants clean and care for them according to their needs. A healthy plant is less likely to attract pests and disease than an unhealthy one.

☐ Use only sterilized soil for your plants.

☐ Examine plants frequently to be sure they have not come under attack.

☐ If you find pests, treat your plants immediately according to the following directions. During treatment, keep the affected plants apart from healthy ones.

Insect	Description	Treatment
Mealy Bugs	White, oval-shaped insects, about ¼ inch long when mature. Have a powdery coat and are found on leaves, stems, and where stems and leaves join. They make nests of white, fuzzy material.	Pick off by hand or by tweezers. Or wash or spray off with soapy or clear water. Or dab with a cotton swab dipped in alcohol. Repeat treatment every few days until pests are gone.

Aphids	Pear-shaped, nearly transparent insects with long legs, about $\frac{1}{8}$ inch long when mature. May be green, black, yellow, brown, pink, or red. Some have wings. They cluster on undersides of leaves or on young leaves and stems or buds.	Treat as above.
Red Spider Mites	Tiny reddish mites, less than 1/50 inch long that leave yellow flecks on leaves and sometimes produce tiny webs that stretch from leaf to leaf. Mites are hard to see but they are visible sometimes on webbing or through a leaf when held up to the light.	Spray or wash with water twice a week until pests are gone.
Scale	Flat insects with shell-like coating, from 1/16 to $\frac{1}{4}$ inch in diameter. They may be white, black, gray, or brown. Scale infest leaves or stems or both.	Wash or scrub off with a toothbrush dipped in lukewarm soapy water. Rinse in clear, lukewarm water.

White Flies	White, flying insects, about 1/16 inch long when mature. Young insects look something like scale and are found on undersides of leaves.	Treat young white flies as above. Spray off mature insects with water or try to clap them between your hands.

Pesticides are used by some people to rid plants of pests, but I don't recommend them. They are dangerous to use and not worth the risk.

The above are the most common house plant pests. Other pests such as cyclamen mites are more difficult to detect and treat. If you suspect your plant is under attack from an insect you cannot identify, or if one of the above have completely taken over your plant, throw it out, soil and all. And make sure that you sterilize the pot immediately.

Some plants are bothered by slugs, snails, sowbugs, earthworms, or millipedes. Remove them if you see them. Earthworms are helpful in a garden but in a potted plant they will disturb the roots.

WHEN YOU GO AWAY

House plants, like pets, can tie you down if you let them. You hear of people who can't vacation because of their plants. Most successful gardeners have developed ways of caring for their plants when they are away.

I read of one man who sticks his plant collection in his bathtub, waters them, and covers the tub with a plastic sheet. This sounds like a good idea to me.

Another technique is to cover each plant or group of plants with a plastic tent. First you water the plants and let them drain. Then you set them on pebble trays and build a plastic tent over the plants and around the pots. Use plastic bags or plastic sheeting. Prop the plastic up on sticks and tuck the plastic under the pots or tray. Be sure the plastic does not press down any leaves. Place the plants out of direct light. You can leave them for up to two weeks under these mini-greenhouses.

Don't set cacti and succulent gardens under tents. Most of them can stand a bit of a drought once in a while. Do remove them from your windows, however, so evaporation and transpiration will not be too fast.

TOOLS FOR THE JOB

You don't need fancy equipment to be a successful indoor gardener. Most of the tools you will need can be found right in your own

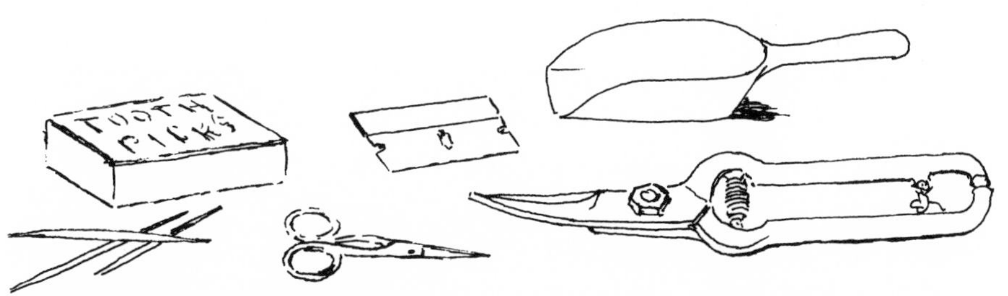

kitchen. Tools specifically designed for raising house plants are convenient, but not necessary.

You'll need something to water your plants with. You'll also need a container in which to mix soil and a spoon or some other tool to use in mixing it. You'll need measuring tools, a digging tool, a shoveling tool, and something sharp to cut with. You'll need things to clean with and perhaps some kind of mister.

Use your imagination when searching for tools. Whatever works is right. Just be sure you keep your tools clean. It also helps to store them all in one spot.

3 *Propagating Your Plants*

To propagate means to make something multiply. Propagating your plants can be half the fun of indoor gardening. It's so much more satisfying to raise a new plant from a seed than to buy one already sprouted.

Most plants can be propagated from seeds or from a cutting of the plant. Seeds can be bought at nurseries or ordered from catalogs. Cuttings can be obtained from your own plants or from friends. It's fun to exchange cuttings. It is surprising how fast you can increase your collection of plants by getting cuttings from others.

One of my friends raises African violets. I'm always after her for a leaf or two from one of them. Someday my collection may be as big and beautiful as hers.

You will need a special type of rooting mixture in which to propagate both seeds and cuttings. Most potting soils are too rich and too heavy. I like to use plain sphagnum moss or plain peat moss for propagating. But any of the following will do as well.

Remember to moisten sphagnum and peat moss before using. Soak in warm to hot water for a few minutes. Then squeeze out and use.

☙ *ROOTING MIXTURES*

USE:

Moistened sphagnum moss

or

Moistened peat moss

or

Coarse sand

OR MIX AND USE:

1 part moistened peat moss

1 part sand or vermiculite or perlite

or

1 part sterilized garden or packaged potting soil

1 part vermiculite

☙ *TO PROPAGATE FROM SEEDS*

You can plant the seeds of most house plants at any time of year. But unless you have a low-voltage heating coil for this purpose, you had better wait until spring or summer. Most house plant seeds require constant warmth to sprout. Winter house temperatures usually fluctuate too much for tender seeds.

Don't expect all your seeds to sprout. Not all seeds are viable—capable of growing. All plants produce some seeds that are sterile. And seeds can be killed in storage.

Many gardeners plant their seeds in containers called flats. Several rows of seeds can be sown at one time in them. They can be purchased at garden centers.

For small jobs, you can use a squat 3-inch pot measured across the top, or a cottage cheese container, or the bottom of a milk carton, or a cardboard tray in which fresh vegetables are often packaged. Just be sure the container you use has a few holes for drainage. I use a can opener for punching holes in cardboard and flexible plastic containers.

Now, here's what you do:

FILL the bottom of your container with broken crockery or pebbles.

FILL the remainder of the container to within ½ inch of the top with a moist rooting mixture.

SCATTER your seeds over the top of the mixture.

COVER the seeds with additional mixture to the depth of their own thickness. The covering will be very thin. If the seeds are extremely small, do not cover at all.

IMMERSE the container in a bowl or basin of lukewarm water. The water should be deep enough so that it can be soaked up through the soil to the surface, but not so deep that it will spill in over the rim. This is called bottom-watering.

REMOVE the container when the water reaches the soil surface.

SET aside to drain.

COVER the container with plastic wrap or a plastic tent.

SET it in a warm spot. Low-voltage heating cables can be used to help germination. These can be placed on window ledges, in trays, or on shelves, wherever propagation is to take place. Place the seed containers right on the cables.

CHECK the propagating mixture from time to time to be sure it is moist. Water to keep the mixture moist but not soggy. Seeds need constant moisture to germinate.

REMOVE the cover from the container once the seeds have sprouted.

MOVE the seedlings to a warm, sunny spot and water regularly, continuing to keep the mixture moist, but not soggy.

THIN the seedlings out so that they are 1 inch apart once they have a second pair of leaves. Use a tweezers to pull out the extra seedlings.

FERTILIZE the seedlings once a week with a very mild solution. It should be about one-half the strength recommended for adult plants.

TRANSPLANT the seedlings to regular soil when they are large enough to handle. Separate them very carefully with a fork so that you do not disturb their delicate roots.

COVER the transplanted seedlings with a plastic tent and set them back in their warm spot.

UNCOVER the seedlings and move them to a display spot in your home when the young plants appear strong and show new growth.

WATER and FERTILIZE according to the directions given for adult plants.

TO PROPAGATE FROM CUTTINGS

A cutting is what it sounds like—a portion of a plant that has been cut off. Propagating plants by leaf or stem cuttings is very popular. This section will deal with stem cuttings, sometimes called slips. Refer to the individual plant chapters for a description of what the stem cutting should look like. Information on how to make a leaf cutting from an African violet, philodendron, and crassula are given in the individual plant chapters. How to propagate by air-layering is covered in the chapter on dieffenbachia.

Cuttings can be rooted in water or a good rooting mixture. I prefer rooting in water when it is possible, as it is the easier way and you can see the roots forming. A succulent should not be rooted in water. It might rot.

Rooting a Cutting in Water

Stick the cutting upright in a glass or jar of lukewarm water, and set it in a warm spot out of direct sun. Roots will form at the bottom of the cutting or at one of its joints within two to six weeks, depending on the plant. Add water to the container as it evaporates.

When a number of roots have formed, plant the cutting in a 2½- or 3-inch pot containing a soil recommended for the plant in its chapter. Try not to disturb the roots more than necessary. Place the new plant in an appropriate spot in your house and care for it as per directions.

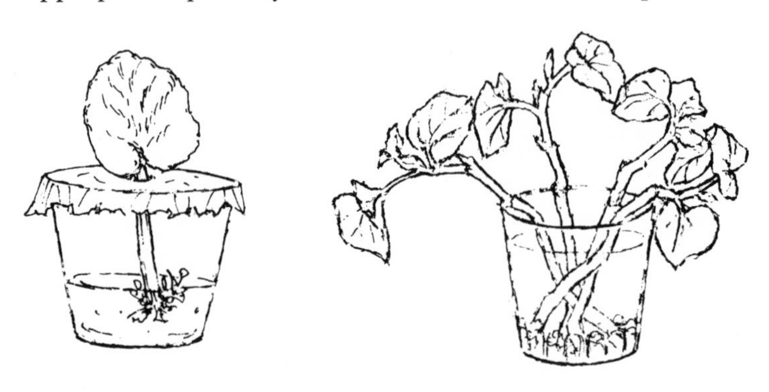

Rooting a Cutting in Soil

PREPARE a pot or other container with a rooting mixture as you would for seeds.

MAKE a hole in the mixture with a pencil or other tool.

INSERT the cutting in the hole and press the mixture gently around it.

WATER the cutting lightly with lukewarm water.

COVER the container with a plastic tent.

PLACE the cutting in a warm spot out of direct sun.

KEEP the propagating mixture moist but not soggy.

BEGIN checking for roots after ten days or so. Gently pull on the cutting. If it gives easily, stick it back in the rooting mixture and try the test again in another week. If it resists a little, it probably has roots and is ready for transplanting.

TRANSPLANT the rooted cutting to a container and soil appropriate for the plant, trying not to disturb the roots more than necessary.

PLACE the new plant in an appropriate spot and care for it according to directions.

Some people dip their cuttings in a hormone mixture to speed up rooting. These preparations are available at plant centers.

Rooting Succulents

Succulents require a slightly different treatment to protect them from rot. Before inserting a succulent cutting into a rooting mixture, allow it to dry out a few hours until a scar forms over the cut. Then hold off watering the cutting for a few days.

HOW TO MAKE A PLASTIC TENT. The easiest way to make a plastic tent over a potted plant is with sticks and a plastic bag. Insert three or four sticks around the inside edges of the pot. Carefully draw the bag over the sticks and tuck its edges in around the bottom of the pot. A sheet of plastic could be used instead of a bag. Clear plastic cake savers, plastic bread boxes, glass jars and even a glass cheese bell also can serve as mini-greenhouses for seeds, seedlings, and cuttings.

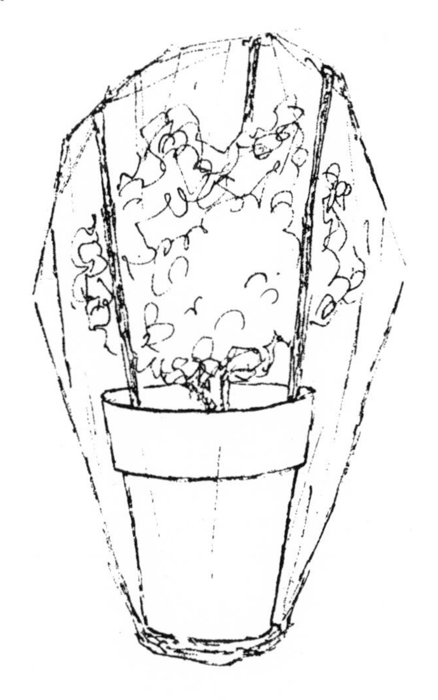

African Violet

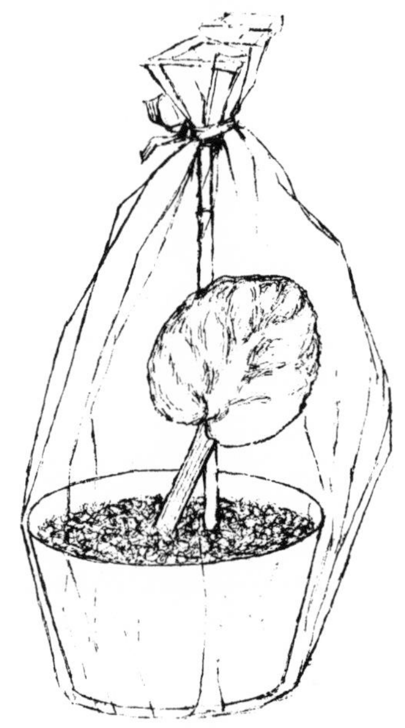

A leaf in rooting material

A leaf in water

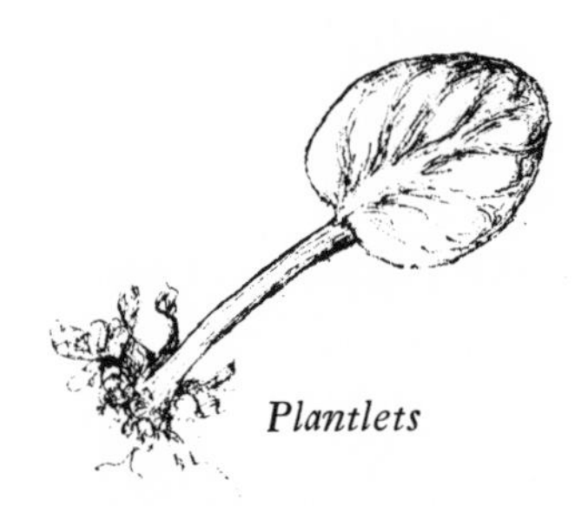

Plantlets

4 *Blossoms and Velvet:* African Violet

LATIN NAME: *Saintpaulia.*
POPULAR NAME: *African Violet.*

Does best in bright light, but not full sun; warm temperatures; high humidity.

Blossoms and more blossoms—that's what African violets are known for. These low-growing plants produce lovely blossoms all year around. Their hairy, velvety leaves are appealing, too.

While there are only a few species of African violets, there are thousands of varieties. New varieties are developed by plant breeders every year. Some have curly leaves. Some have rounded leaves. Some have blossoms of only a few petals. Others have plump, fluffy, ruffly ones with many petals. Blossoms come in many colors—white, blue, purple, pink, and combinations. I have had best luck with white, blue, and purple ones. These seem easiest to grow. Your florist will be able to help you select a hardy, ever-blooming variety.

As its name implies, the African violet is native to the continent of Africa. It was first discovered and collected in Tanganyika, now Tanzania. Wild African violets grow in the shade of jungle trees in forested hills and mountains. But the African violet is not really a violet at all, although some varieties do have a violet-like blossom.

African violets are discussed first in this book because the book is arranged in alphabetical order, and also because they are probably the most popular of all flowering house plants. They have a reputation of being a bit tricky to grow, though, so I would not make them my first plant. I find that they are easy to grow and very hardy. The trick, if there is one, is finding the right place for them.

☙ *ENVIRONMENT*

Location

You must find the right spot for your African violet if you want it to bloom. Climate is most important to the plant. The three essential factors are light, temperature, and humidity.

In general, a warm east or west window (away from a radiator) is the best year-round spot for this plant, but other spots will work, too, if you make them. The plant likes a south window in winter, for instance. But in summer the midday sun will be too strong for it. During the summer an African violet in a south window would need a shield. If a tree partially shades the window, you are in luck. Otherwise, sheer curtains or bamboo shades can be drawn at midday between the plant and the window. Or you can place the plant away from the window on a piece of furniture.

I have seen African violets doing nicely in a large north window. But I wouldn't try this location unless you are willing to take a gamble.

The African violet needs daytime temperatures of 68° to 75°F. Most house climates fall within this range. At night the plant should not be subjected to temperatures lower than 60°F. This is where you might run into problems. Many windows get quite cold at night in winter. If you live in a frosty area, don't even try a window ledge without a storm window, and in any case, plug up cracks between the window and the sill. Then, at night, move the plants out of the window to a warmer place in the room. Or protect your plant from chill in one of the ways suggested on page 25.

African violets enjoy humidity. Set them on pebble trays if you can.

Container

Most people raise African violets in clay or plastic pots. Planters and terrariums also can be used. A terrarium fashioned out of a fish bowl makes an excellent, humid home. Careful watering and good drainage should be provided.

You don't want to put an African violet in too big a pot. Put a seedling in a 2½-inch pot. Put a young plant in a 3-inch pot. I always repot young nursery plants into 3-inch pots. Mature plants with a 7- or 8-inch leaf span do best in 5- or 6-inch pots.

A leaf resting against the wet rim of a clay pot can rot. Coat the rims of your clay pots with paraffin wax. (Heat the paraffin. Dip the pot's rim into it. Let the paraffin harden. Then redip.) Rims also can be covered with a strip of aluminum foil.

Soil

The African violet needs a rich, porous soil—one that drains well, provides plenty of oxygen for the roots, and is rich in humus. Use one of the high-humus potting soils suggested on page 15.

CARE

Be gentle when watering, potting, washing, and otherwise handling these plants. The succulent-like stems snap very easily.

WATER to keep soil moist, but not soggy. Don't be misled into overwatering by the fact that the plant likes humidity. Soggy soil is a different matter completely and will quickly rot the plant. My plants in 3-inch pots need water about twice a week. Use only lukewarm water. It is particularly important to use a can with a long spout or a long-necked syringe when watering African violets. You want to avoid getting leaves and the plant crown (center) wet. Cold water left on leaves may spot them. If any drops fall on the leaves, blow or carefully brush them off immediately.

MIST African violets with a fine lukewarm spray frequently—daily or, if you can, more often.

FERTILIZE, as with most house plants, once or twice a month with a mild solution. In winter, don't fertilize if your plant becomes dormant. Plants should be fed only when they are growing vigorously.

TURN plants frequently to promote straight growth.

REMOVE damaged leaves and faded flowers. Cut them off near the stalk with a sharp knife or pull them off gently.

Clean leaves once a month or so by brushing gently with a fine soft brush. If the plant looks dirty, wash the entire plant in soapy water as described on page 32. Be extremely gentle so as not to snap off any leaves.

Guard your plant against window chill in winter.

Remove any side shoots (called suckers) that appear on the trunk. These shoots can be rooted to produce new plants. An African violet should be grown with a single crown only.

Repot your plants into larger pots when they become pot-bound—about once a year. Set those with extra-long trunks more deeply in the soil. Otherwise, plant at the old depth. Do not pack soil around the plant heavily. African violets like a light, well-aerated soil.

☙ *PROPAGATION*

African violets can be propagated by seed, by leaf cutting, and by division. Growing seeds requires the patience of Job, so I recommend one of the other methods. A seed may take months to sprout, and during all that time the germinating seed needs regular care.

To propagate by leaf cutting, select a medium-sized healthy leaf. Cut the leaf and its stem from the parent plant using a sharp knife or razor blade. Leave about 2 inches of stem attached to the leaf blade. Insert the cutting at an angle into rooting mixture just deep enough so that it will stand up. Toothpicks can be used to prop up heavy leaves. Cover the pot with a plastic tent as described on page 40. Check occasionally to be sure the rooting mixture remains moist.

Small shoots will appear at the base of the cutting within two weeks to two months. When the new leaves are about one-third the size of the parent leaf, remove them from the potting mixture. Shake off loose soil. Separate the plantlets by pulling them gently away from the parent leaf. Plant in soil and return them to a plastic tent until growth begins again. Remove the tent and place the new plants in an appropriate spot.

You also can root a leaf in water. Cut as above. Stick the leaf through a piece of aluminum foil or waxed paper and set it in a jar of lukewarm water. Set it aside out of direct sun. Roots will form in a few weeks. Plantlets will appear at the end of the stem in a few more weeks. When they are about 1 inch long, plant them (still attached to the parent leaf) in a rooting mixture. Separate the plantlets and transplant to soil when the leaves are one-third the size of the parent leaf, as above.

Divide a plant if it develops several crowns. Let the potting soil dry out a bit beforehand and shake some of it off the roots. Gently pull the crowns apart. Plant the crowns in 3-inch pots and cover with a plastic tent until new growth begins. Put the plants in potting soil, not a rooting mixture.

Remove suckers or side shoots that develop along the main trunk by cutting off with a sharp knife or razor blade. Root them as you would a cutting.

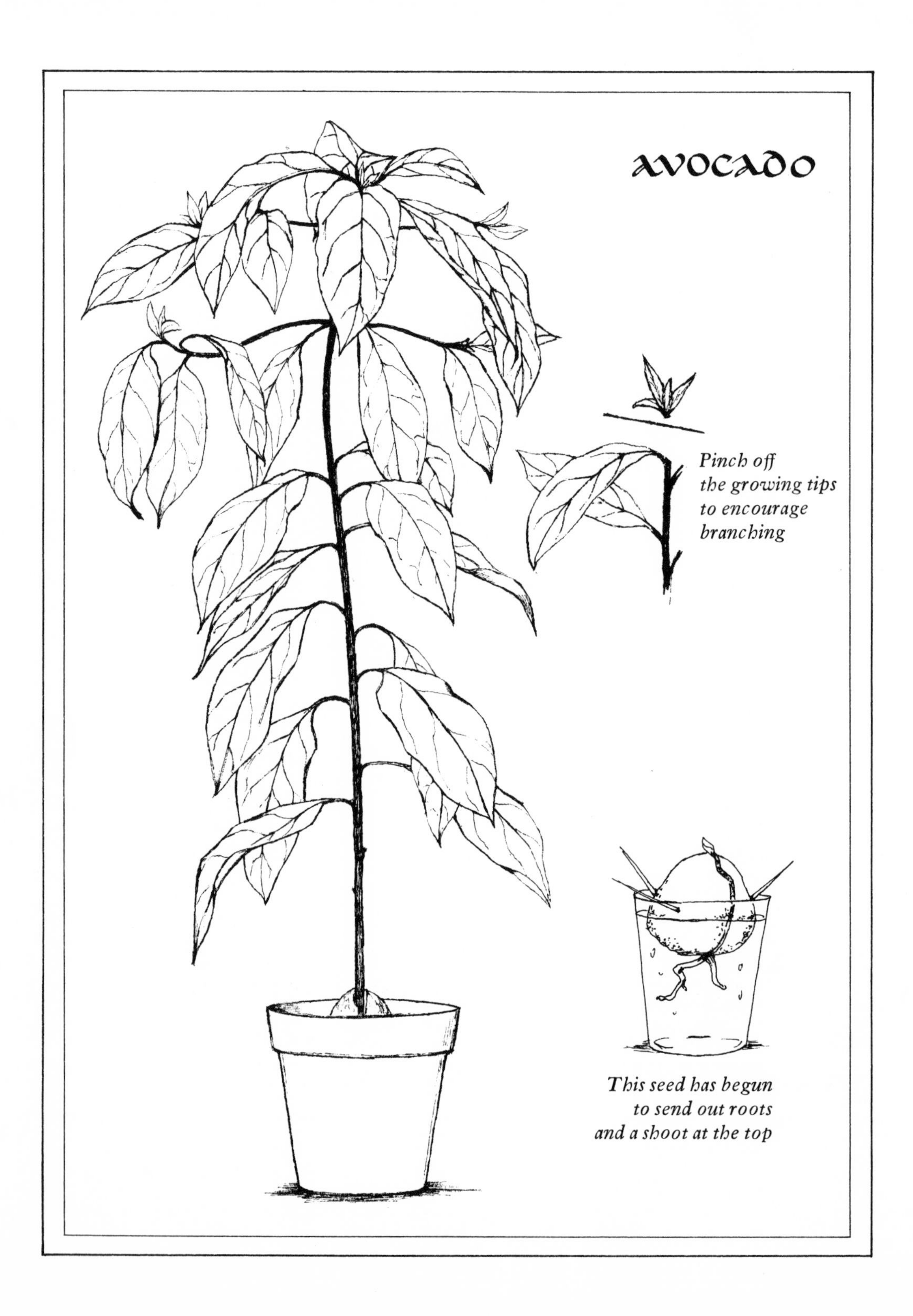
avocado
Pinch off
the growing tips
to encourage
branching
This seed has begun
to send out roots
and a shoot at the top

5 *Potted Pit:* Avocado

LATIN NAME: *Persea americana, Persea drymifolia.*
POPULAR NAMES: *Alligator pear and Avocado pear.*

Does best in full sun; warm temperatures; moderate humidity.

You can make a room look like a jungle very cheaply with several avocados. All you have to do is talk your family into eating a lot of these delicious, high-calorie fruits. Then plant the pits (seeds). The plants that result can live in your house for several years if given proper care and a good environment.

You can let the plants grow naturally—into skinny trees. Or you can prune them drastically to raise bushier plants.

When I was a girl living in Southern California, it seemed that everyone had an avocado tree in the back yard. The sunny climate was perfect for the tree. Great orchards of avocados dotted the countryside. I was sure the avocado was a native California tree. But not so. The avocado is native to neither California nor Florida, the two places where it is cultivated in the United States. It is more tropical in origin, coming originally from Mexico and parts of South America.

In their native habitat, certain mature avocado trees grow to heights of 40 to 60 feet. Leaves are deep green and shiny and range from 4 to 12 inches long. Blossoms are small and greenish. Because of the many varieties of avocado, the fruit varies in shape and size.

The tree commonly grown in Florida bears a pear-shaped fruit with a pimply skin. Undoubtedly, it was this species which gave the avocado the nickname, "alligator pear." The California species has a more rounded, smooth-skinned fruit.

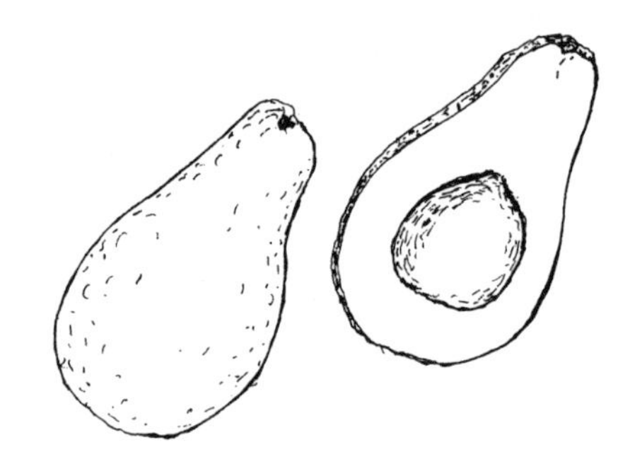

Raised indoors, it is doubtful that the plant will bear fruit. But a house plant transplanted to the outdoors may bear fruit in time, if conditions are right.

◆ *ENVIRONMENT*

Location

The avocado will do best in a warm, sunny spot, preferably in a south window. Without adequate sunlight, growth will be slow and disappointing. Some growers recommend putting the potted tree outside in a protected spot in summer.

Container

You'll be rooting your avocado in water, so use anything for this—a tumbler, a jar, a vase, or a plastic cup. Just be sure it is ½ inch or so larger than the pit.

Transplant the rooted seed to an 8- to 10-inch pot. When the tree is about 6 feet tall, move it to a tub or other large container. Good drainage should be provided.

Soil

Use one of the all-purpose or sandy potting soils suggested in Chapter One. The soil should come up just to the top of the seed.

☙ *PROPAGATION*

A friend complained to me that she couldn't get an avocado seed to grow. She tried and tried over many months with many seeds, but nothing happened. It turned out that she was placing her seeds upside down. Turn the pointed side of the seed (small side) up, and it's very easy to get an avocado going. The seeds can be rooted in soil or water. I prefer working in water as it's easier to see what is going on.

SELECT a ripe avocado (gives a bit when you press it between thumb and finger). It should not be mushy, bruised, or rotting. If a ripe fruit is not available, choose a healthy-looking hard one. Let it ripen at home in a warm place. Do not store an avocado in the refrigerator.

REMOVE the seed from the ripened fruit and peel away as much skin as will come off easily.

WASH it in warm water; dry; and wipe clean.

INSERT three or four toothpicks into the top one-third of the seed (pointed or small end).

SUSPEND seed in a container, using the toothpicks as supports.

FILL the container with lukewarm water to cover the lower half of the seed.

PLACE the container in a warm, dimly lit spot until roots and top growth form. (First top growth will be only a pointed stem coming through a split in the seed.)

ADD water (lukewarm) to container to maintain water level.

At this point you have a choice. If you want a skinny plant:

TRANSPLANT now to pot and soil, being careful not to injure the roots. Leave the top of the seed exposed. Place pot in a sunny place.

PINCH out the top leaves when the plant has six full leaves.

If you want a bushier, fuller plant:

KEEP seed in water until the main stem grows to 6 or 7 inches, but move to a sunny spot.

CUT off stem at midpoint with a scissors, razor blade, or sharp knife. The remaining stem will now be 3 inches long or so. (Growth will stop temporarily, perhaps for a few weeks.)

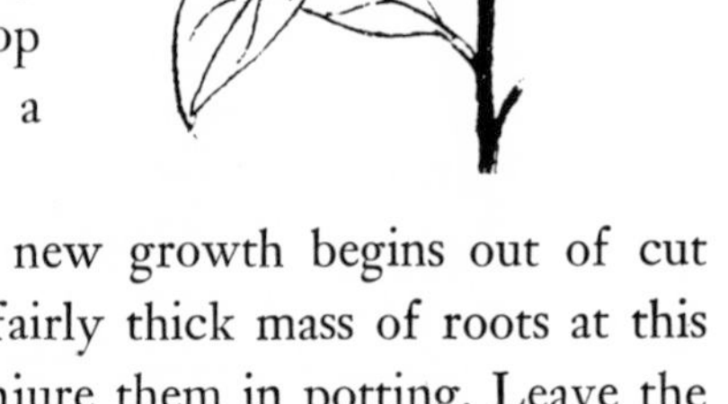

TRANSPLANT to pot and soil when new growth begins out of cut stem. There should be a fairly thick mass of roots at this point. Be careful not to injure them in potting. Leave the top of the seed exposed.

Some seeds will produce two or more stems. Leave the secondary (smaller) stems alone and pinch out or cut back only on the main stem.

Not all seeds are viable. Some will not grow no matter what you do. It's always wise to have at least two seeds going at once to insure success. If a seed hasn't begun to root after six weeks, or if the water is cloudy, throw out the seed and begin another.

CARE

WATER to keep soil moist, but not soggy. Do not let the soil dry out completely or the plant will wilt. Many avocados require daily watering.

Fertilize, as with most other house plants, once or twice a month with a mild solution.

Clean leaves once a month or when dusty by spraying or sponging off.

Turn plant frequently to help insure straight and even growth.

Guard your plant against window chill on cold winter nights.

Prune plant continually by pinching or cutting back top and sides to promote balanced and bushy growth. Pinch back the new top growth when plant reaches 2 or 3 feet. Do this whether or not you cut the plant back while it was still in water. If side growth gets lopsided, pinch out branches on the heavy side. The plant has a tendency to branch unevenly. If any branches get out of control and ruin the plant's appearance, cut them off at the main stem. Don't be afraid to take drastic measures to keep the plant looking bushy or balanced. Avocados are vigorous growers and will not be harmed by continual pruning.

Insert a 3-foot bamboo stake or wooden dowel for support along the side of the plant when top growth begins to get heavy. This will be when it reaches a height of 18 inches or so. The stake should be inserted to the bottom of the pot about 2 inches away from the main stem. Attach the plant loosely to the stake with a string or twist-tie. As the plant grows, sagging branches may be loosely tied to the stake for support. Replace the stake with a longer one as the plant outgrows it.

Transplant the plant to a tub when it has outgrown its pot and begins to look silly in it. This may be when the plant reaches a height of 6 feet. Continue providing a stake for support until the plant is mature and strong.

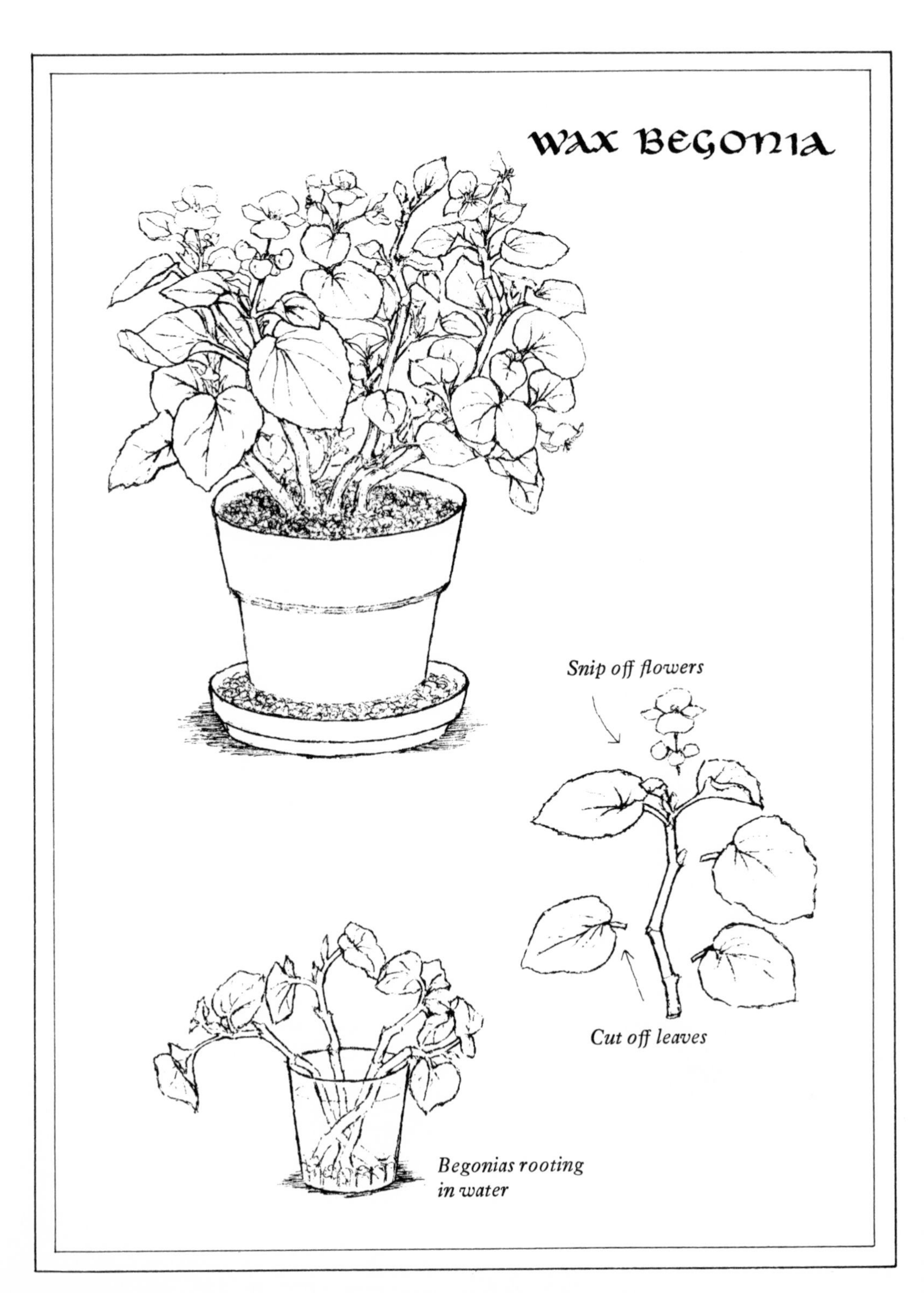
WAX BEGONIA
Snip off flowers
Cut off leaves
Begonias rooting
in water

6 *Hardy Translucence:* Wax Begonia

LATIN NAME: *Begonia semperflorens.*
POPULAR NAMES: *Wax Begonia, Fibrous-rooted begonia.*

Does best in partial to full sun; medium to warm temperatures; moderate humidity.

Next to the African violet, the wax begonia is probably the most popular indoor flowering plant. *Semperflorens* means everblooming. These beautiful plants put out lots of small cheery blossoms all year.

The blossoms come in white and shades of red and pink. Some are delicate looking and nearly transparent. Others are fuller and look like tiny roses. Double-flowered varieties have longer lasting blooms.

Wax begonias also have attractive leaves. They look somewhat waxy, giving the plant its nickname. Leaves range in color from bright and dark greens to an almost iridescent brown.

More than 1,000 species of begonia occur in tropical and subtropical countries throughout the world. The wax begonia is native to Brazil. It is the easiest to grow. It does not require as much humidity as other tropical plants. And being slightly succulent, it can survive a short period of drought every now and then.

ENVIRONMENT

Location

An east window is probably the best year-round spot for wax begonias. They like sun but can't take the hot afternoon sun of a south window in summer. A west window suits these plants, too, as well as a bright spot near a window. In winter, begonias will do fine in a south window.

The begonia does not need a high amount of humidity. But it benefits from a place on a pebble tray during extremely dry periods. Keep begonias away from radiators and hot water pipes. They do well in average house temperatures but might wilt under excessive heat. The begonia can take night temperatures down to 50°F, but it prefers temperatures a little warmer.

Container

Keep begonias a little cramped—in what plant experts call a tight pot. In large pots they will not bloom well and are subject to rot. This doesn't mean begonias don't need moving on to larger pots as they get large. But it does mean that you should keep them in pots smaller for their size than your other plants. Be sure the pots drain well.

Soil

The begonia does well in a light, porous soil. Use one of the high-humus potting soils recommended in Chapter One. Don't pack soil tightly about the plant. The begonia needs light packing so that its roots can get plenty of air.

☙ *CARE*

WATER only when the top of the soil feels dry. The begonia requires watering less often than you would imagine for a tropical plant. Too much water rots them quickly. Don't let the soil get bone dry, however, or the plant will wilt.

FERTILIZE, as with most house plants, once or twice a month with a mild solution.

Clean leaves once a month or when dusty by spraying or sponging off. If the plant looks dirty, wash the entire plant in soapy water as described on page 32. The begonia stems snap off easily so use care when handling.

Turn plant frequently to help insure straight growth.

Pinch off growing tips to keep the plant bushy and to produce longer-lasting blooms. If the plant gets leggy and straggly or if its leaves begin getting smaller, prune the plant back to a foot or less. Make your cut right above the spot where a leaf joins the stem. In time new side growth will appear.

Remove faded flowers to promote more blooms.

❧ *PROPAGATION*

The wax begonia is easy to propagate from a stem cutting in water or a rooting mixture. The cutting should be a few inches long. Cut the stem right at a leaf joint. Snip off the bottom few leaves so that three or four remain at the top of the cutting. Remove any blooms.

These plants also can be propagated by seed or root division. Only plants with several stems can be divided. Take a sharp knife and cut between the stems clear through the roots. Pot the divisions in regular soil. Don't be alarmed if the shock of the cutting kills part of the plant. Just remove the damaged parts and carefully tend to the plant until it revives.

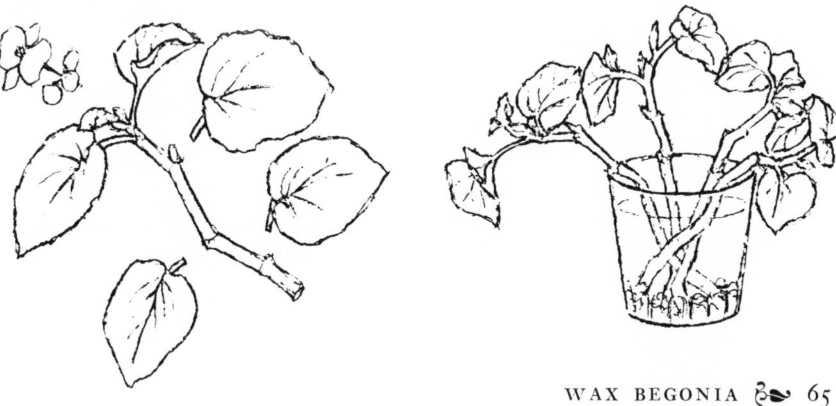

DESERT CACTI

Old Man

Column

Prickly pear

Barrel

Peanut cactus

Beaver tail

7 *Nature's Pincushions:* Desert Cacti

Here are the Latin and popular names of a few popular desert cacti: *Cephalocereus senilis, Mexican old man; Chamaecereus silvestri, Peanut cactus; Platyopuntia, prickly pear; Ferocactus acanthodes, Barrel cactus; Opuntia basilaris, Beaver tail; Cereus peruvianus, column.*

Do best in full sun; medium temperatures; low to moderate humidity.

If you're a person with only a little time to spend on gardening, a desert cactus is for you. It will require very little care. In fact it seems to thrive on neglect.

There are perhaps as many as 1,200 species of cacti. They come in a variety of shapes and sizes—tall and skinny, short and fat, tree-like, barrel-like, button-like, and snake-like. Nearly all desert species come armed with tufts of stiff, sharp spines.

Cacti are succulent plants. Succulents are a group of plants that have developed a way of surviving without water for long periods of time. They have thick stems which hold water and thick waxy skins which keep water from evaporating quickly. They can live off their stored water for weeks. During longer periods of drought, say during winter months, they go into dormancy (a resting period) where they can go without water for months. Succulents have widely spreading roots that absorb water quickly so that they can take advantage of any rains that fall.

As you might suspect, most cacti are found in dry regions or areas that experience long dry spells. Not all cacti are desert plants, however. Some come from tropical climates. They are more difficult to raise and are not discussed here.

Cacti are New World plants. They are native to North and South America. They can be found as far north as Canada and as far south as Chile and Argentina. The greatest number of cacti grow in Mexico, in our Southwest, and in dry parts of the Andes Mountains.

You have probably seen pictures of our southwestern deserts dotted with blooming cacti in spring. Most cacti put out blossoms that are quite brilliant. I am always thrilled when any of my cacti bloom, for it is a great treat to have these plants bloom indoors. Just the right conditions are needed, right amount of water and light, so don't expect blooms. Cacti make interesting house plants, with or without blossoms in spring.

Cacti are available at nurseries and most garden centers. Most desert species are endangered and, therefore, should not be gathered from the wild.

☙ *ENVIRONMENT*

Location

Most cacti require a good deal of sun. Put your cactus in full sun, unless otherwise directed by your florist.

During the short days of winter, cacti go through a resting period when they don't grow. You may move them to a dimmer spot at this time if you wish to free your window for some other use. A rest in a dim spot without much water may help your cactus to bloom.

Some cacti can withstand a good bit of cold. But be on guard. If your cactus is damaged by frost, remove it from its window position or protect it from window chill at night.

Some young cacti will burn if the sun gets too hot. Set them back from the window a bit.

Container

A cactus needs a pot with perfect drainage. Being a succulent, it cannot stand wet feet. It is set up to store water. Standing in water will overtax the plants water storing ability and rot it at its base. So pot your cacti in containers with large holes and a thick layer of crockery or pebbles at the bottom. A smallish pot, one just big enough to hold the roots and support the plant, is best. In general, the pot should be no more than an inch wider than the cactus it holds.

I prefer clay pots for cacti. They lose water quickly and their earthy color sets a cactus off most pleasingly.

Dish gardens, where several plants are arranged together, are popular habitats for cacti. Pains must be taken to provide good drainage and a minimum of water must be given. Consult Chapter Fifteen for instructions on how to make a dish garden.

Soil

Cacti need a quick-draining, porous soil. Use one of the sandy soil mixtures recommended in Chapter One.

◆§ *CARE*

WATER regularly throughout late spring and summer when the top of the soil feels dry. During winter months most cacti become dormant. Water sparingly during these resting periods. Gradually withhold water beginning in late fall. By midwinter you should be watering no more than once a month—just often enough to keep the cactus from shriveling. Water only on bright days when water evaporates quickly. Watering too often during winter may rot your plant or force it into unhealthy growth. Remember this: A cactus is naturally equipped to withstand periods of drought. Overwatering is the main cause of cactus death.

FERTILIZE occasionally with a mild solution during spring and summer, but no more than once a month. Do not fertilize during the fall and winter rest period.

CLEAN plants once a month or when dusty by spraying with water or brushing with a soft brush. Spray only on sunny days when water evaporates fast. Return the plant to a sunny window only after it is completely dry, or it may burn.

REPOT your cactus each spring in fresh soil. If it is root-bound, repot to a larger pot. Otherwise, return it to its old pot which you have scrubbed clean.

HOW TO HANDLE CACTI. Some cacti have fierce spines that can inflict painful skin pricks. When handling these, wear heavy gloves or use tongs. Some people hold the plants in a wad of newspaper, as well, but I find this technique cumbersome.

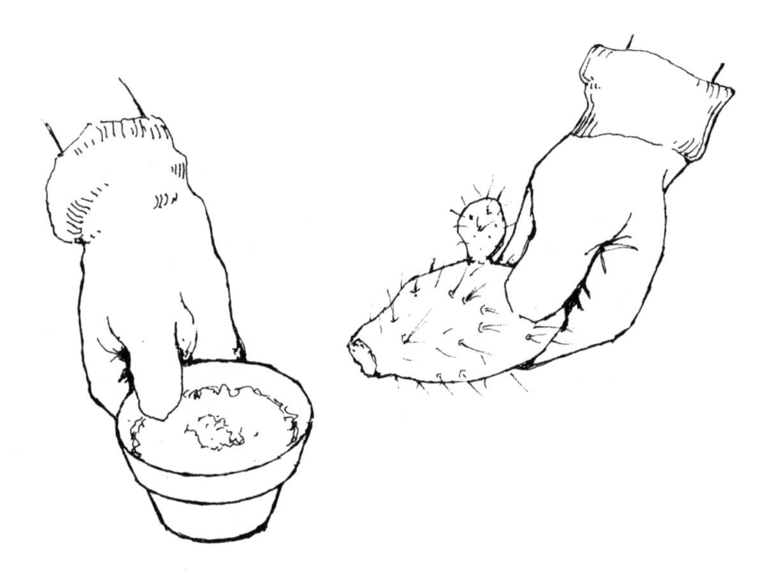

☙ *PROPAGATION*

Most cacti can be propagated from seed. The catch is that many nurseries sell only packages of mixed seed so you won't know which cacti you are getting. Cacti are slow growing and seedlings take a long time to grow, too.

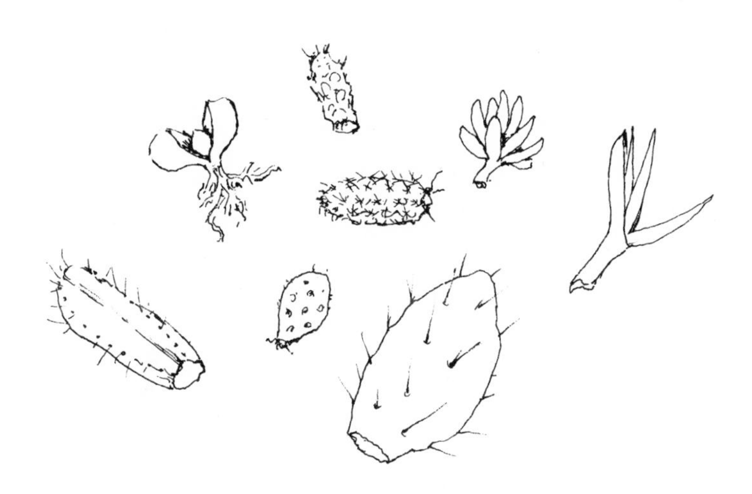

Many cacti can be propagated by division. A cacti with more than one stem coming up from the ground can be done this way. Slice between the stems with a sharp knife and cut right on down through the roots. Each plant division should have some roots. Let the wounds dry out and scar over by setting the divisions aside for a day or two. Then pot the divisions in a sandy soil.

Other cacti produce small little infant plants which grow off a stem or around the base of the plant. Cut these off with a sharp knife; let dry out for a day or two; then root in a rooting mixture. When the infant plant, or sucker, forms roots, transplant it to sandy soil.

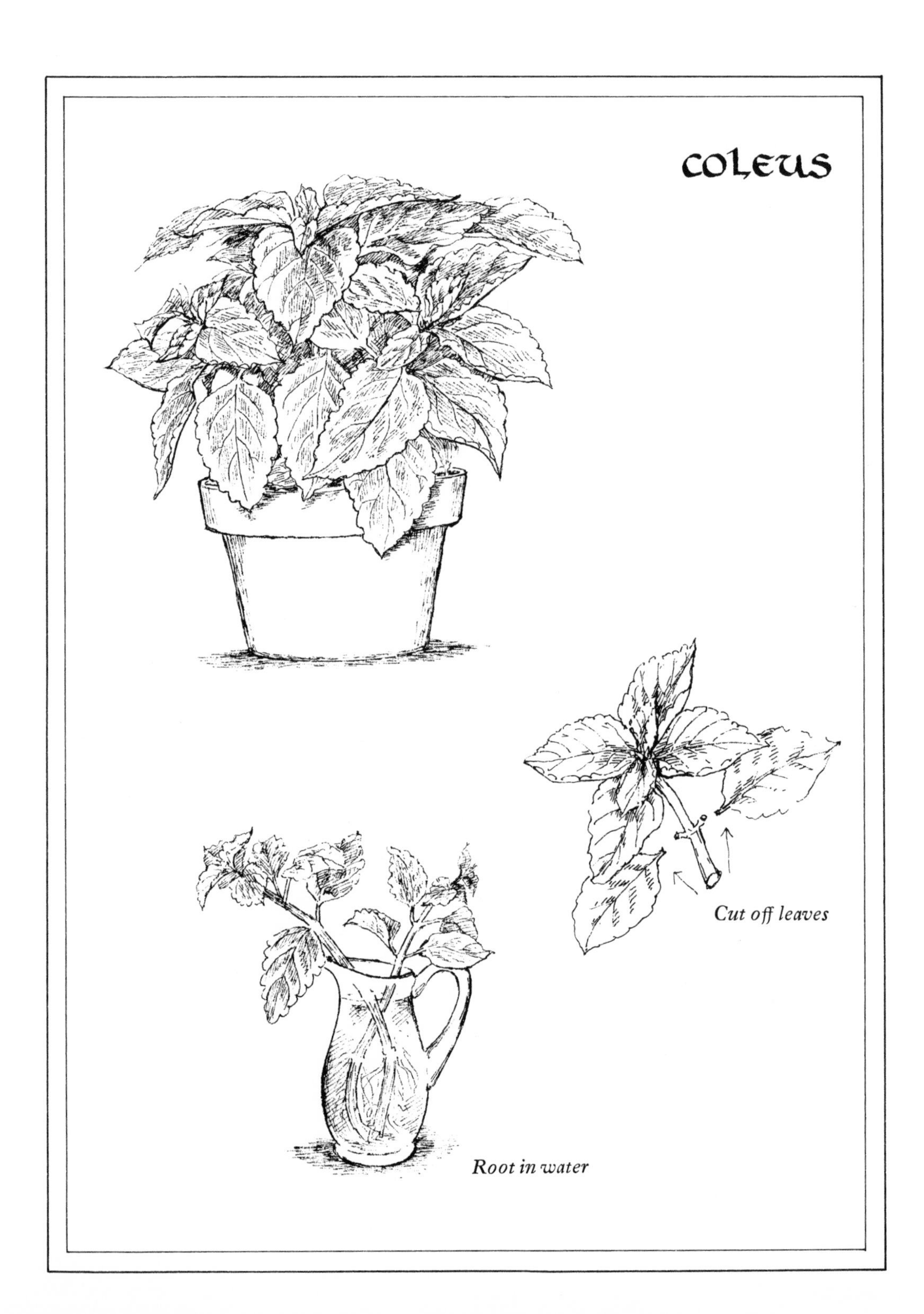
COLEUS
Cut off leaves
Root in water

8 *Leaves of Brilliance:* Coleus

LATIN NAME: *Coleus blumei.*
POPULAR NAMES: *Coleus, Foliage plant.*

Does best in full sun; cool to medium warm temperatures; moderate humidity.

To me, the coleus is among the friendliest of house plants. It is an old-fashioned favorite that anyone can grow as long as he or she has a sunny spot. Its colorful leaves give a window a bright and cheery appearance on even the coldest winter days.

I have a large coleus that is more than five years old. My husband and I started it from a seed when we were living in a small apartment in New York City. Even though we had only one large, north-facing window, we were able to keep the plant growing. Now, with a sunny window to grow in, it has become a grandparent plant many times over. I have given dozens of cuttings from it to friends who have in turn given away cuttings from their plants.

There are two species of coleus. The common one, *Coleus blumei*, came originally from the island of Java. *Coleus rehneltianus*, a creeping plant, comes from the island of Ceylon.

Coleus breeders have produced a vast variety of plants with leaves in combinations of pinks, reds, purples, yellows, and greens. In spring the plant produces a tall, blue flower. Although the flower is somewhat unremarkable, it does remind one of certain wildflowers found in fields throughout the country.

⁂ *ENVIRONMENT*

Location

Coleus needs sun to retain leaf color just as many sun-loving green-leafed plants do. Without enough sun, the leaves do not produce enough food. Undernourished leaves become dull or turn yellow.

Put the coleus in full sun during winter. During summer months, coleus also will do well in the light of an east window.

The coleus can get along in almost any house climate—cool or warm, moist or dry. I would avoid putting one right over a radiator, however. I would avoid a stuffy spot, as well. The coleus seems to need good ventilation, or it droops badly.

Container

You can put your coleus in just about any container. One with a drainage hole is best.

Soil

I have found that the coleus can live in just about any kind of soil—even soil taken right out of a garden. An all-purpose potting soil is generally recommended. Use one of those suggested in Chapter One.

⁂ *CARE*

WATER coleus frequently to keep the soil evenly moist, but not soggy. The coleus is a thirsty plant. Small plants may need daily watering. Try not to let the soil dry out completely between waterings. The thin leaves of the coleus cannot store water and the plant wilts easily if denied water. Don't be overly alarmed if your plant wilts, however. You will see that it will revive quickly as soon as it is watered.

FERTILIZE, as with most house plants, about once or twice a month with a mild solution.

CLEAN leaves once a month or when dusty by spraying with lukewarm water.

MIST your plants regularly if it is in a very dry spot. Otherwise misting is not necessary.

TURN plant daily to keep leaves from turning toward the sun and turning their undersides to you.

PINCH out tops to promote bushy growth, especially with young plants.

MOVE your plant in the spring to a protected area outside, if you can. The plant seems to gain strength with this treatment. Be sure to water it frequently.

PROPAGATION

You can grow coleus easily from seeds or stem cuttings. The coleus is a fast grower.

I find it easier to root stem cuttings in water. The cutting should be a few inches long with four to six leaves on the stem. (Pinch off blossom, if present.) Cut the stem right below a leaf joint and remove the bottom leaves.

Plantlets grow at the base of leaves

Remove the bottom leaves. Let the cutting dry out before inserting it in the rooting material.

9 *Strength and Succulence:* Crassula

LATIN NAME: *Crassula argentea.* Called *Crassula aborescens* by some florists.
POPULAR NAME: *Jade plant.*

Does best in partial sun; cool to medium warm temperatures; low to moderate humidity.

You often see crassulas in dish gardens with other plants. They are favorites with florists. But watch out. A mature crassula can be a giant—up to 4 or 5 feet tall.

Actually, the plant is slow-growing. A mature, tree-like crassula may be as much as twenty-five years old, so you really don't need to worry about its outgrowing a pot too quickly.

Crassulas are succulents. They are native to South Africa. They grow chiefly near the Cape of Good Hope where they are found in rocky, often dry places. Like all succulents, crassulas can live through long droughts.

I have always had crassulas. They are easy to care for and always handsome in clay containers. Crassulas seem to be able to withstand almost every kind of neglect and mistreatment except watering too frequently, which you have probably gathered is the chief enemy of most house plants.

ENVIRONMENT

Location

Ideally the crassula should have a spot in bright light. An east or west window is best. But the crassula can survive without good light for months at a time. So a bright north window is all right, too, as well as a spot away from a window, especially during the winter. Cut down on water and fertilizer when the plant is out of bright light and don't expect it to grow much.

Container

I prefer clay pots for all succulents, and the crassula is no exception. Because of its shallow root system, the plant does best in a shallow pot. Be sure to provide a good layer of crockery or pebbles on the bottom for drainage. If you don't have a shallow pot, fill a regular pot at least one-third full of drainage material.

Soil

The crassula will do best in a quick-draining soil that is rich in organic material. Follow one of the suggestions for sandy soil in Chapter One.

CARE

WATER when the soil feels dry. In spring and summer, when the plant is actively growing, this may be as often as with other house plants. In winter, the plant's growth slows down and so should your watering. Overwatering will produce a spindly and unattractive plant or may kill it.

FERTILIZE regularly with a mild solution during spring and summer, but not more often than once a month. Cut down on fertilizer in the fall. In winter, when the plant is dormant, do not fertilize at all.

CLEAN leaves once a month or when dusty by spraying or sponging off. Every so often bathe the leaves with soapy water and rinse well.

TURN the plant frequently to promote straight and even growth.

PRUNE as the plant gets large to keep it balanced. An unbalanced plant may get top heavy and fall over. Cut off out-of-control branches at a joint with a razor blade or sharp knife. Propagate the cuttings. Pinch young plants to promote branching.

REPOT or PLANT the crassula in fairly dry soil. Follow the directions for potting succulents on page 23.

PROPAGATION

The crassula can be propagated by leaf or stem cutting and by seed. I prefer taking stem cuttings.

The cutting should be a few inches long with a few leaves left at the tip. Cut below a joint with a razor blade or sharp knife. Remove the bottom leaves and let the cutting dry out a day or two before inserting in a rooting mixture.

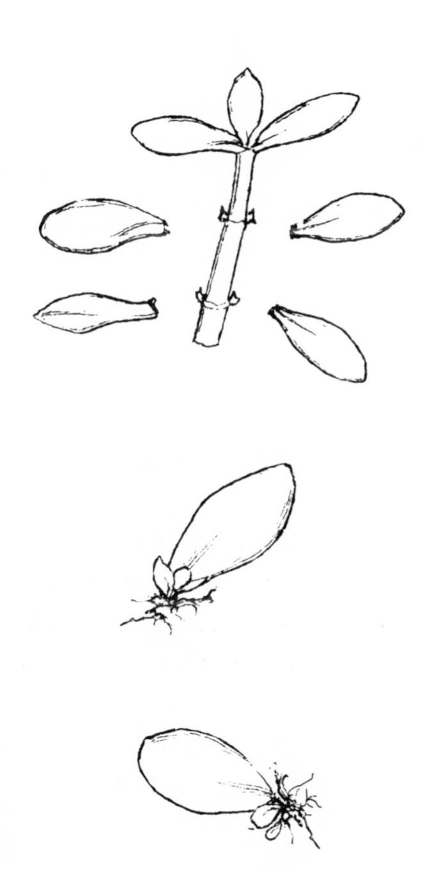

To propagate by leaf, merely break or cut off a large, healthy leaf. Let it dry a day or two. Then insert it at an angle in a rooting mixture and keep damp. Roots will begin forming at the base of the leaf in a few weeks. A tiny plantlet will appear later. Transfer the plantlet to a pot and sandy soil when it is big enough to handle.

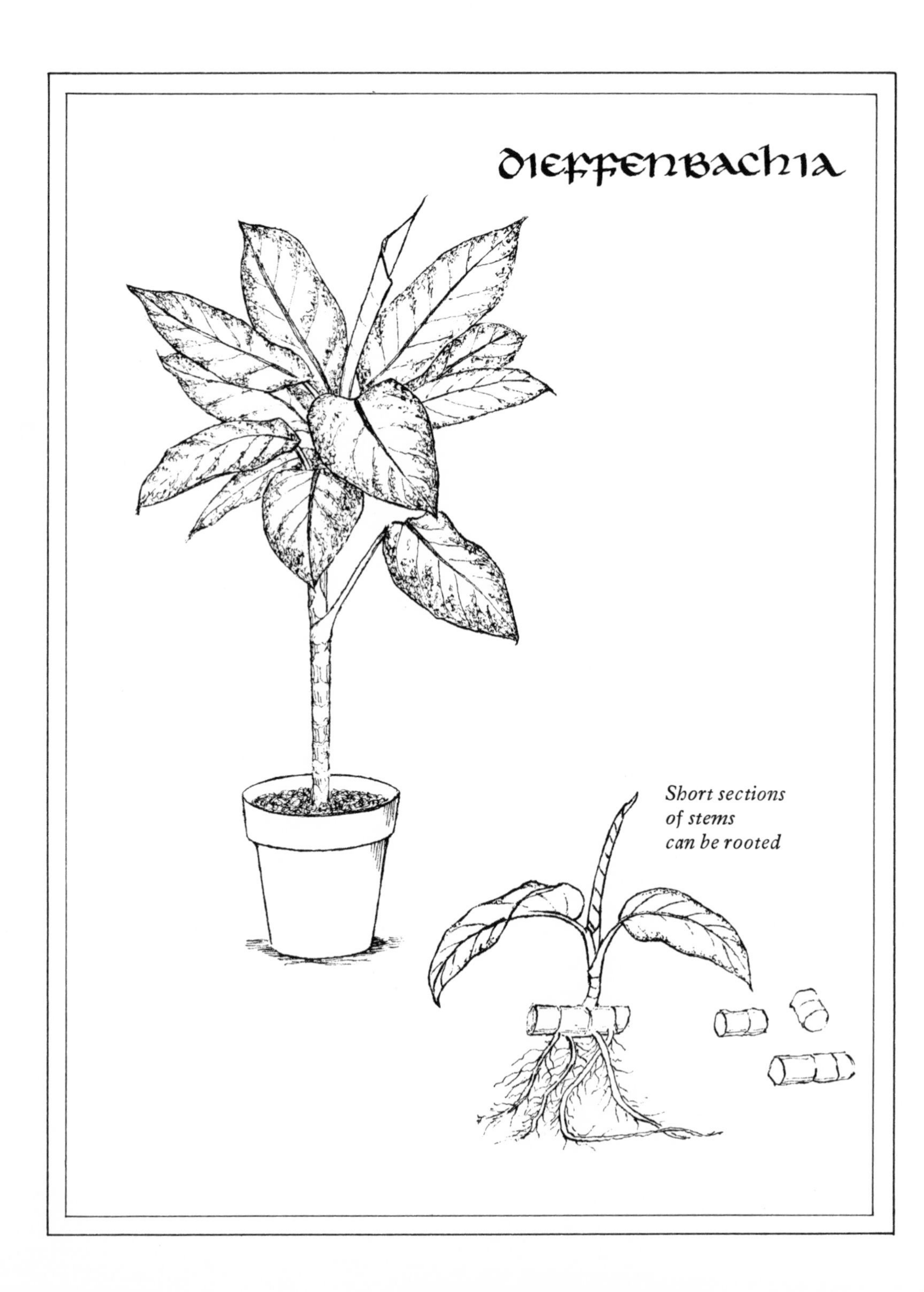
DIEFFENBACHIA
Short sections
of stems
can be rooted

10 *Tall on a Cane:* Dieffenbachia

LATIN NAME: *Dieffenbachia picta.*
POPULAR NAME: *Dumb cane, Mother-in-law's tongue.*

Does best in partial sun; medium to warm temperatures; moderate humidity.

Are you looking for a plant that will get big enough to fill an empty spot in your room? The dieffenbachia may be the answer. It grows to a height of about 4 feet and has large, handsome leaves. They are speckled with white. A mature dieffenbachia looks very nice by itself in a tub. It also makes an attractive backdrop to a plant grouping.

There are eighteen or more species of dieffenbachia. *Dieffenbachia picta* is the best known and most popular. It is native to Brazil. It is hardy and will grow almost anywhere in your house. It can even take dim light and can stand a certain amount of neglect.

As dieffenbachia mature, they develop a thick cane-like stalk. Some mature plants will drop their bottom leaves, retaining only a tuft of leaves at the top.

The dieffenbachia is mildly poisonous if eaten or put in the mouth. It is doubtful that you or a family member would ever bite into the plant, but a word of caution is in order. Never put a dieffenbachia, or any non-food plant, in your mouth.

☙ *ENVIRONMENT*

Location

The dieffenbachia can grow just about anywhere, in shade or in bright light. I would avoid placing the plant in a really dim spot as its leaves will darken. And I would avoid a spot in full sun as its leaves may burn. Otherwise, any place in the house will do as long as it is moderately warm. I have one in a north window, one in a shaded south window, and one back from an east window. When I lived in California, I had a large one toward the center of a room.

The dieffenbachia enjoys moist air, but it can survive in a dry house. I have seen these plants growing in dry cleaning plants, which must get very dry. And I have a healthy one growing very close to a radiator. I do mist it regularly, however.

Container

A large dieffenbachia looks nice in a bucket or wooden tub. But just about any container will do. These plants also do well grouped with other plants in planters. You often see them used in decorating offices.

For young plants use any kind of pot with good drainage.

Soil

One of the all-purpose potting soils mentioned in Chapter One will suit this plant fine.

☙ *CARE*

WATER when the soil approaches dryness.

FERTILIZE, as with most house plants, once or twice a month with a mild solution.

Clean leaves once a month or when dusty by spraying or sponging off. Bathe the plant in soapy water from time to time and rinse well.

Mist with lukewarm water if plant is set near a radiator or other extremely dry spot.

Turn the plant frequently to promote straight growth.

Guard against window chill during winter months.

Remove bottom leaves as they turn yellow. The yellowing of bottom leaves is normal.

Air-layer the plant if it becomes too tall and lanky. (See directions below.)

❧ *AIR-LAYERING*

Air-layering is a way of reducing the length of a plant's stem to improve the plant's looks. It is also a type of propagation. Mature dieffenbachia plants that lose their bottom leaves look ungainly. Air-layering will give them a compact look again.

The procedure is not easy. So only try it if your plant looks terrible. And then don't be crushed if your project fails. Accomplished gardeners sometimes have trouble air-layering. But if your plant *needs* air-layering, don't be afraid to try.

Cut a notch in the stem 2 to 6 inches below the bottom leaves or at a point that would make stem and leaves look in proportion. Eventually you will cut through the stem at this notch.

Place a stick behind the notch to brace the stem, if necessary, and tie in place.

Stuff moistened sphagnum moss into the wound to keep it from scarring over and then surround the wound and entire stem with more moistened sphagnum moss. In a pinch you might be able to use shreds of paper towels instead of the moss.

WRAP a plastic bag or piece of plastic wrap around the moss and tie it at top and bottom. If plastic is applied properly, you will not have to keep opening it up and moistening the moss.

SET the plant in a warm spot and water as usual.

REMOVE the plastic wrap from time to time and moisten the moss, if necessary. The moss should not be allowed to dry out.

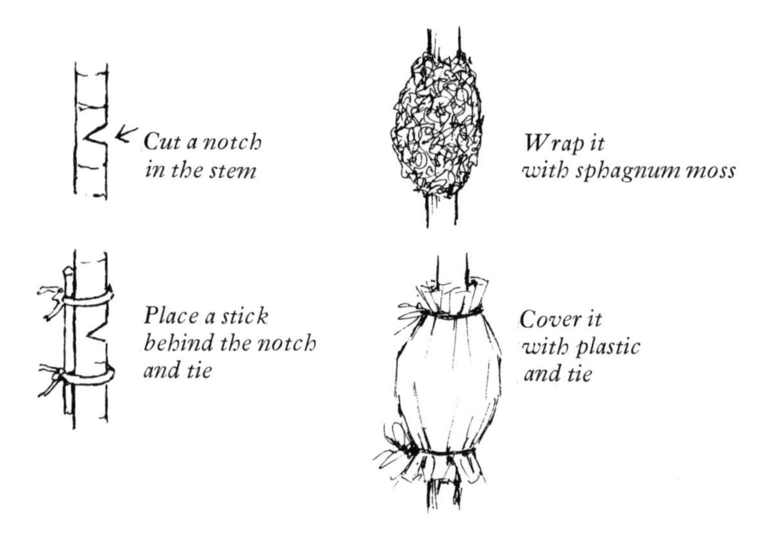

REMOVE the plastic wrapping when roots have formed around the notch. This will occur in eight weeks or so. You will be able to see the roots poking out through the moss.

CUT through the stem below the new roots and pot the rooted top portion in an all-purpose potting soil.

CONTINUE to care for the old plant and water it sparingly. A new plant may form at the base of the old stem in time.

PROPAGATION

Most gardeners do not attempt propagating dieffenbachia. But it can be propagated in a number of ways, all involving severing the plant with a sharp knife or razor blade.

The plant can be air-layered as described above. A cutting also can be made of the top and rooted in soil or water, although I have never had luck with this procedure.

Another way to propagate a lanky plant is to cut up the long cane into 2- or 3-inch segments and root these. Each segment will produce a new plant. Make the cuts at joints along the stem. Then lay the segments on moistened rooting mixture. Cover with a thin layer of additional mixture and set in a warm spot. I use a low-voltage heating cable to provide warmth, but you can do without it if you have a spot that is constantly warm. Water to keep the mixture moist as you would for any other kind of cutting. New plants will come up at the joints of the stems. Pot the new plants, stems and all, when they are a few inches tall.

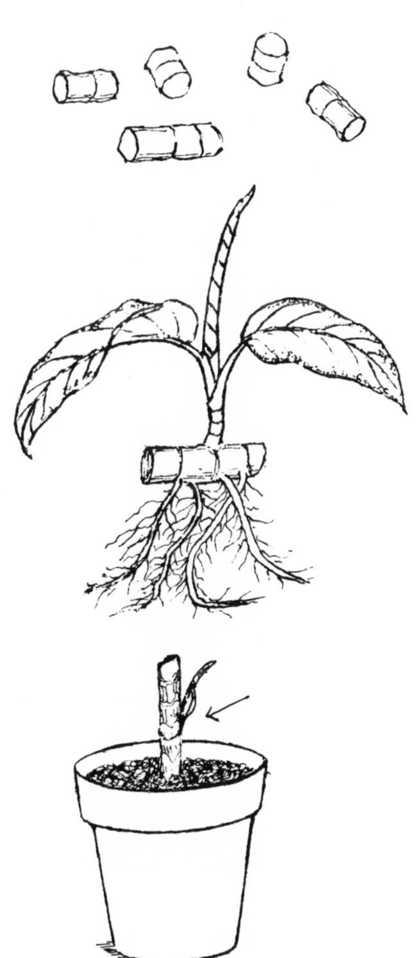

After "beheading" a dieffenbachia, don't throw away the remains of the old plant. A new plant may form at base of old stem.

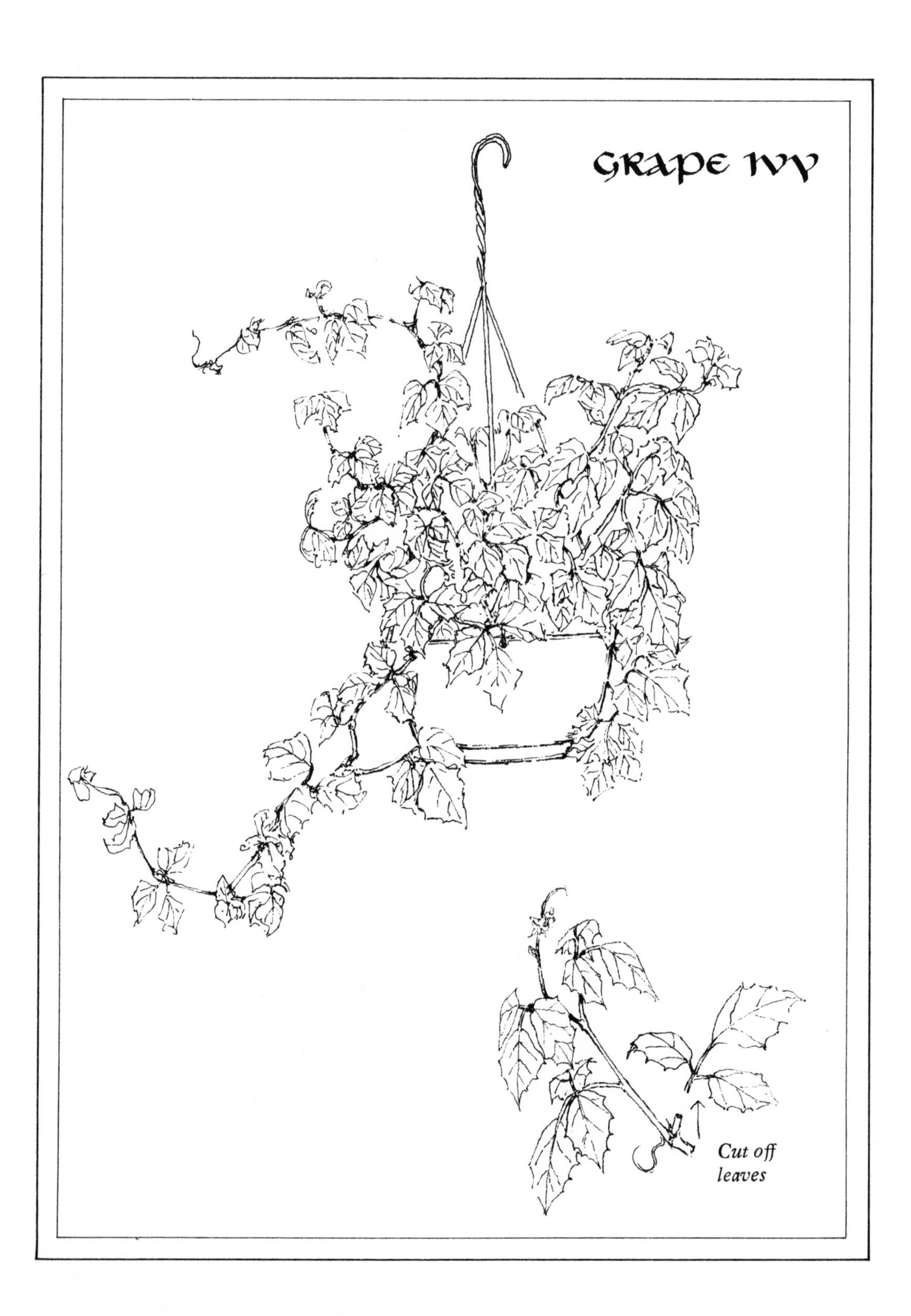
GRAPE IVY
Cut off
leaves

II *Indestructible Climber:* Grape Ivy

LATIN NAME: *Cissus rhombifolia.*
POPULAR NAME: *Grape Ivy.*

Does best in partial sun; cool to medium temperatures; medium to high humidity.

Hardy and indestructible—these are words often used to describe this climbing plant. It can be raised "in impossible places," say the experts. This means in dim parts of a room, in any window, and in most temperatures. High heat and burning sun are probably its only enemies.

I have to agree. I can truly say that the grape ivy is one plant that has never failed me. For this reason it shall always be a resident in my home, filling spots that are unfit for other plants.

The grape ivy has glossy, sometimes paper-thin dark green leaves. The leaves grow in groups of threes, reminding some people of poison ivy. The plant is native to northern South America and the West Indies.

There are a number of *Cissus* plants. They are not related to the English ivy and the other common ivies, but like these plants, the grape ivy and other *Cissus* plants can be trained around windows and look well in hanging pots.

⁂ *ENVIRONMENT*

Location

Put this plant just about anywhere but in full sun or excessive heat. You can train it to grow around a window or up a pole or trellis, as well as to hang from a pot. It will do well in dimly lit spots, but of course don't stick it in a closet. All plants need some light.

Container

Grow the grape ivy in any container. It is safest in a container with good drainage but young plants can be placed in dish gardens and terrariums as well. As with all climbing and trailing plants, it looks handsome in a hanging basket.

Soil

Use one of the all-purpose potting soils recommended in Chapter One for the grape ivy.

⁂ *CARE*

WATER to keep the soil evenly moist, but not soggy. The grape ivy is not particular about how it gets watered. If in doubt about when to water it, however, lean toward keeping it more dry than wet.

FERTILIZE, as with most house plants, once or twice a month with a mild solution. If the plant is in a dim spot where it isn't growing rapidly, fertilize less frequently.

CLEAN the leaves once a month or when dusty by spraying or sponging off. Bathe the plant in soapy water occasionally and rinse well.

MIST the plant daily in winter if your house is very dry. The plant will survive without misting, but it will be more supple and attractive if not allowed to get too dry.

PINCH off growing tips from time to time to keep the plant symmetrical and bushy unless you are training it to climb.

PROPAGATION

The grape ivy is easy to propagate from a stem cutting. The cutting should be 3 or 4 inches long with a few leaves at the end. Cut below a joint with a razor blade or sharp knife. Remove the bottom leaves. Root the cutting in water or a rooting mixture.

Heartleafed Philodendron

A leaf bud cutting inserted into rooting mixture

A stem cutting rooting in water

12 *In Darkness and in Light:* Heartleafed Philodendron

LATIN NAME: *Philodendron oxycardium.* Called *Philodendron 'cordatum'* by many florists but the true *P. cordatum* is a large plant.
POPULAR NAME: *Heartleafed philodendron.*

Does best in partial sun; medium to warm temperatures; moderate to high humidity.

In a dentist's office, on a teacher's desk, in a barber shop, over a mantel—you run across this climbing philodendron everywhere. It is the most widely sold of all house plants. And for good reason. *Philodendron oxycardium* is inexpensive, easy to come by, and attractive. It will grow in just about any light. It can survive poor soil, improper watering, and neglect. To flourish, however, it requires proper care just as all house plants do.

There are many species of philodendron, and most make good house plants. The heartleafed philodendron is native to Central America and the Caribbean Islands. Philodendron means "tree-loving." In its native jungle habitat, this plant lives in the shade of trees, the trunks of which it climbs in search of light. It has clasping roots which cling to bark. It is accustomed in nature to enduring dry and wet seasons, plus high and low temperatures. This is why it is such a hardy, indoor plant.

ENVIRONMENT

Location

Grow this plant anywhere! The philodendron will do very well in a place just out of direct light, for example, on a table near a bright window. But it will also do well in a north window, completely away from a window, or on a mantel. It can live in both dry and damp rooms and in cool or warm ones. I have grown philodendrons in bathrooms, kitchens, bedrooms, and living rooms—even in hallways. Do keep it out of direct sun, though.

Some people train these philodendrons to grow upward around shady windows. The plants also look well in hanging baskets or hanging down from a pot on a shelf.

Container

The philodendron has a very small root system so it does not need a large pot. One just big enough to support it will do.

When philodendrons are placed on furniture they are often provided with a support made of bark which is inserted into the pot. The plant is trained to grow up the bark. Consult the section on training plants in Chapter Two.

The philodendron can also be put in dish gardens, terrariums, and hanging baskets.

Soil

Use one of the all-purpose or high-humus potting soils suggested in Chapter One for this plant. Its roots like air so mix in extra vermiculite if you like.

CARE

WATER to keep the soil just damp, not soggy. You do not need to let the soil dry out between waterings but the practice will not hurt the plant.

FERTILIZE, as with most house plants, once or twice a month with a mild solution. Use fertilizer less often if the plant is placed in very dim light.

Clean leaves once a month or when dusty by spraying or sponging off. Bathe the plant in soapy water occasionally, if it gets dirty, and rinse well.

Pinch off growing ends occasionally to produce a bushier plant. If your plant gets straggly, improve it this way: Place the plant in a larger pot with new soil. Wind the long branches around on the top of the soil. Pin the branches down every few inches with paper clips or hair pins. Be careful not to trap the leaves between the stems and soil as you do this. Bring leaves over stems. New roots will form at the places where the branches are pinned and the plant will look bushier and healthier.

Mist your plant if it is in an extremely dry spot to keep it supple and attractive. The clinging roots cannot grasp well if they become dry and brittle.

PROPAGATION

The heartleafed philodendron is easy to propagate by stem or leaf bud cuttings. Root a stem cutting in water or a rooting mixture. Root a leaf bud cutting in a rooting mixture.

A stem cutting should be a few inches long with two to four leaves on the end of the stem. Cut the stem about ½ inch below a leaf joint. Remove bottom leaves.

To make a leaf bud cutting, cut a piece of stem which has a good size leaf off the plant. Leave a piece of stem about ½ inch long above and below the place where the leaf joins the stem. Insert this stem section in rooting mixture.

SWEET POTATO

Bottom scar

13 *Kitchen Cast-off:* Sweet Potato

LATIN NAME: *Ipomoea batatas.*
POPULAR NAMES: *Sweet potato, Yam.*

Does best in full sun; warm temperatures; moderate humidity.

Here's a fast-growing vine you can grow for next to nothing. Ask your mother to pick up a few extra sweet potatoes (sometimes called "yams") on her next trip to the market. She'll hardly notice the money spent and you'll have many hours of fun ahead of you.

Sweet potato vines are easy to grow. You can grow them in soil or water and train them to grow around a window or up a homemade trellis. But there is one hitch. You must find a viable potato, one that is healthy and able to sprout. Be sure to consult the section on selecting sweet potatoes before buying one.

The sweet potato is not related to the common potato. It is a member of the morning-glory family of plants. But like the Irish potato, it is a valuable food plant. The edible part is an enlarged root. There are many varieties of sweet potatoes. What supermarkets call a "yam" is a variety with a rather moist meat. A true yam is a different plant.

Sweet potatoes are native to the East Indies but are now widely cultivated throughout the world. In the United States the plant is grown as far north as New Jersey, but it is cultivated chiefly in the cotton-belt states.

⁂ *ENVIRONMENT*

Location

Once your sweet potato has begun to sprout, it will need lots of sun and warmth. A place in a south window would be the best as a year-round spot. An east or west window would work in spring and summer but would not be so good during the short days of winter.

Sweet potatoes prefer temperatures in the 70s and should not be subjected to temperatures much below 60°F. These plants are easily damaged by cold.

Container

Once the plant has sprouted, put it in a large container. One that is about 1½ times as deep as the potato's length is recommended. If you plan to grow the plant in water, use a large quart-sized jar, vase, fish bowl, or other container. An old teapot would make a handsome container for this purpose. Keep the water "sweet" with a few pieces of charcoal. Charcoal for indoor gardening is available at most garden centers, or from a pet store. Do not use charcoal briquets as they contain a chemical binder which is not good for plants.

Soil

The sweet potato requires a soil with good drainage. Use an all-purpose or sandy potting soil which is recommended in Chapter One.

⁂ *PROPAGATION*

SELECT a good sized, plump potato that is free of rot, mold, or black spots. If a few pink buds are showing, great. Your potato has already begun to sprout and probably will grow readily. Avoid buying a sweet potato that has been stored on a refrigerated produce stand. The sweet potato is easily damaged by cold.

BUY your potato between late summer and early winter. These are the best times for propagation. Sweet potatoes are harvested in late summer and fall. They are then heat cured and stored so that they can be sold throughout the year. Your chances of propagating a sweet potato are greater if the potato is young. Older potatoes may have been damaged by improper storage, or may be diseased. I have successfully sprouted potatoes bought in March, but I have had a lot of failures at this time, too. By March a potato may be six months old or older.

SET your sweet potato aside for a few days in a warm spot, unless it already has buds. This will promote sprouting.

SUSPEND the potato with toothpicks in a large container of lukewarm water. The end that was attached to the mother plant, the stem end, goes up. Immerse only one-third to one-half of the potato. (You can recognize the stem end by closely inspecting the potato. A flat scar of maybe a ¼ inch remains where the potato was broken or cut from the mother plant. This side is often, but not always, the blunter end. I once tried to root a potato with the wrong end up. A few buds sprouted but that was about all. Then, discovering my mistake, I immersed the opposite end in water. As if by magic the plant sprouted overnight and began growing profusely.

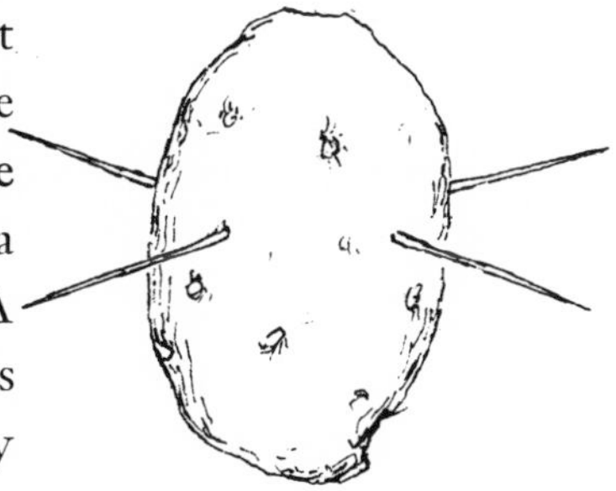

PLACE the container in a dim place until roots and sprouts appear. This should be within a few weeks.

MOVE the potato to a warm, sunny spot at this point, keeping it in water, or

PLANT the sprouting potato in soil. If you prefer, you can let the potato remain in water until growth is five or six inches high, or

TAKE the new sprouts from the potato when they are no less than four inches high and root them. By doing this, you can get several plants from the same sweet potato root. Pull the sprouts off the potato and root them in a rooting mixture as you would root a stem cutting or sucker. If the sprouts have already formed roots, so much the better. When the sprouts start growing, transplant them to an all-purpose or sandy potting soil.

CARE

WATER regularly with lukewarm water to keep the soil moist, but not soggy. You can wait to let the top of the soil just begin to dry out before watering, but don't let it get bone dry.

FERTILIZE, as with most house plants, once or twice a month with a mild solution when the vine is fairly mature. A young vine will be receiving nutrients from the mother sweet potato root. Sweet potatoes propagated directly from the sprouts should be fertilized from the beginning as with any new plants.

GUARD against window chill in winter.

SNIP off all but the three or four healthiest stems once the plant starts growing vigorously.

TRAIN the vine to grow up a support—strings tacked up and around a window or a trellis of some type. Use twist-ties or pieces of string for attaching the vine. In time the vine will attach itself by encircling the string as it grows.

Note: If you are growing the plant in water, add lukewarm or room temperature water to the container as water evaporates. Snip off secondary vines and train main growth as above.

The Terrarium

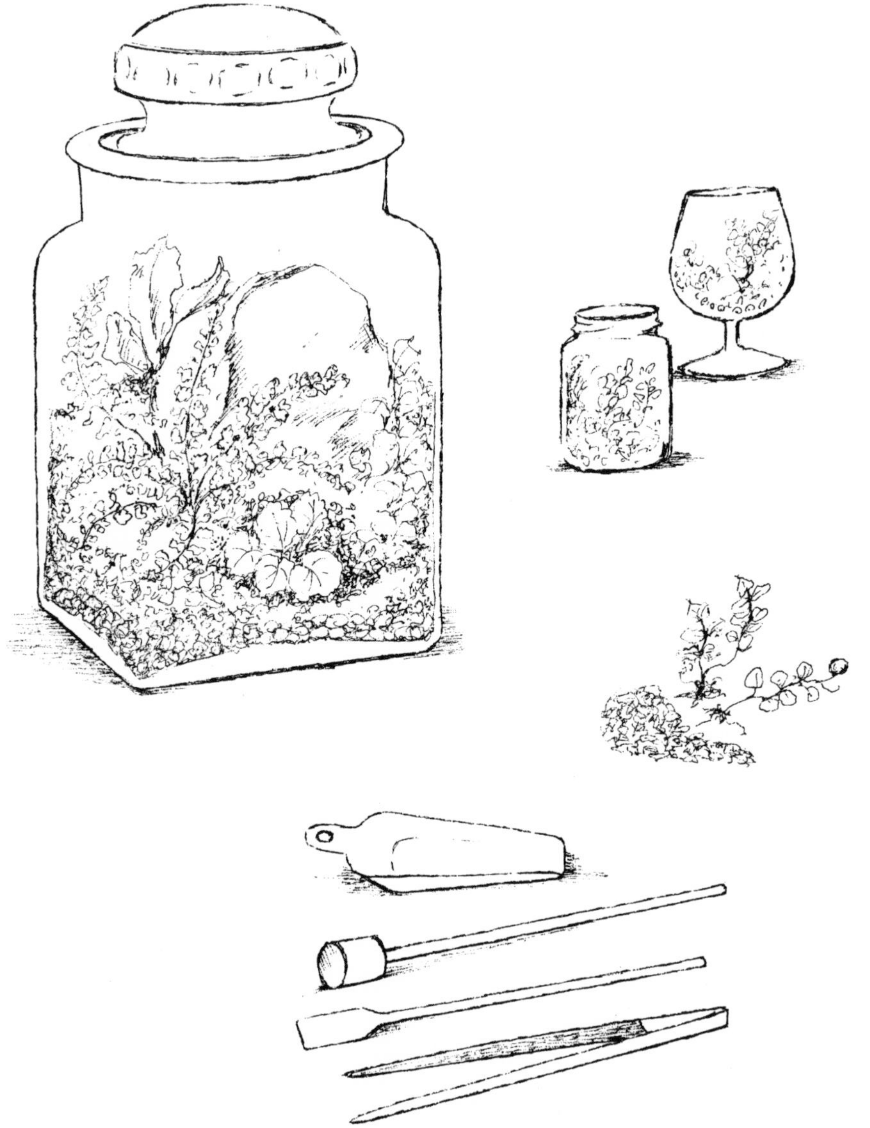

14 *Mini-Environments Under Glass:* The Terrarium

Does best in bright to dim light, but never direct sun; cool to medium temperatures; provides its own humidity.

It is so much fun to construct a terrarium I don't know why more people don't have them. And they are so easy to care for. They are truly the answer for someone who doesn't like to water plants.

Terrariums are gardens under glass. Usually they are composed of tiny plants arranged to look like a natural landscape. A well-done terrarium can be a piece of art.

I particularly like to use tiny woodland plants which I have collected myself. But terrariums can be made up of any group of plants that like moist conditions. Many people use miniature tropical house plants in terrariums.

A successful terrarium needs very little, if any, watering. Moisture is cycled between soil, plants, and air much as it is in nature.

Plants take in water through their roots. They give off (transpire) water through their leaves. In a terrarium the water vapor given off by the plants becomes moisture in the air. The moisture condenses to form droplets of water. These fall upon the soil like rain and are absorbed. Water is again available to the plants. The cycle repeats itself over and over. The water is used and reused. New water is needed only if some escapes into the air of the room.

☙ *ENVIRONMENT*

Location

Place a terrarium of woodland plants in a fairly shady or dimly lit spot. A place in a north window would be perfect or a place set back a little from an east window. If you have a bright room, you can set the terrarium away from a window on a piece of furniture.

Situate terrariums of tiny house plants in a spot appropriate to the plants you are using. A terrarium containing an African violet, for instance, would need a fairly bright spot, say one in an east window.

Container

You can make a terrarium in any glass or plastic container that holds water and lets in light. One that is wide enough at the mouth to let in your hand is easiest to work with. Fish bowls, aquariums, large-mouthed jars, and large brandy goblets are often used.

You will need a cover for your terrarium. Use a piece of glass or a piece of plastic wrapping.

Soil

Use one of the all-purpose potting soils recommended in Chapter One for most terrariums.

☙ *SELECTING THE PLANTS*

Select tiny plants of different heights, shapes, and textures, but with similar needs.

Suitable house plants would be: small maidenhair ferns, African violets, begonias, philodendrons, pothos, wandering Jews, dracaena, palms, ivies, and aralias. Ask your florist for other suggestions.

If using woodland plants, take them all from one area or type of area. Use a small trowel or fork to pry them up. Try to get as many roots as possible with each plant. Carry them home in a plastic bag and keep moist until you're ready to plant. Lichens, mosses, small ferns, ground pines, and other tiny plants that hug the forest floor work nicely together and are attractive. Be on the lookout for small moss or lichen-covered rocks or wood to add interest to your terrarium.

When gathering wild plants, you should be aware that some are endangered and protected by law. Consult your state conservation agency or local horticultural or garden society to be sure. And try not to damage or disturb other plants as you collect your own. It would not make sense to spoil the beauty of a woods while trying to create beauty in a terrarium.

CONSTRUCTING THE TERRARIUM

It helps to have agile hands when making a terrarium. But anyone can do a passable job with a little patience and care. One word of caution: try to keep the terrarium walls clean as you work. It is very difficult to clean the inside of a terrarium once soil and plants are in place.

WASH your container in soapy water; rinse with clear water; and dry well.

PLACE a layer or two of drainage material at the bottom. A layer of pebbles mixed with a few chunks of charcoal covered by a layer of clean, coarse sand is excellent. Or use just the pebbles or only the sand, and add a few pieces of charcoal. The charcoal will keep the terrarium soil from becoming sour.

SHAPE the layers of drainage material into a landscape of hills and

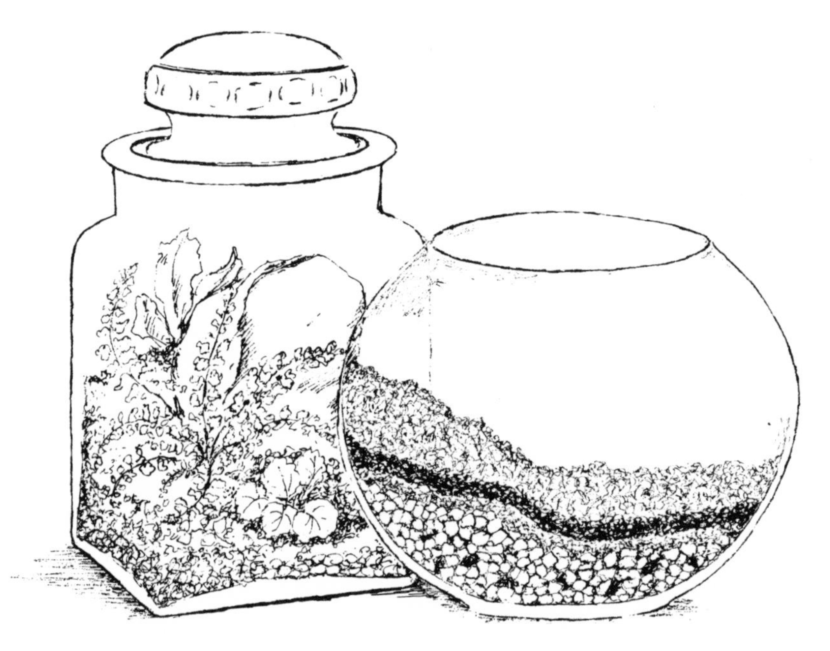

valleys if your container is large enough. This will make your terrarium look more interesting.

Cover the drainage material with a thin layer of moistened peat moss. Over this place a thicker layer of moist all-purpose potting soil. The peat moss will keep the soil from settling into the drainage material.

Arrange the plants in the soil, placing the tallest plants in the center and the shortest plants around the outside. Mosses make a nice border around the outside. Merely press lichens, mosses, and other plants with short root systems into place. Prepare small holes for plants with longer roots. Insert the plants in the holes and lightly press the soil around the plants.

Add an attractive rock, a piece of lichen-covered wood, a sea shell, or pottery object for interest, if you like.

Brush off any soil from the leaves and walls of the terrarium.

Sprinkle or spray the plants and soil with lukewarm water.

LET the water evaporate off the sides of the terrarium.

COVER the terrarium with a sheet of glass or a piece of plastic film.

PLACE the terrarium in bright or moderate light, depending on the needs of the plants being used. Do not place it in direct sun or the leaves may be scorched.

CARE

WATER only if the soil begins to look dry, using a long syringe, sprinkler, or mister. Do not water if the sides of the terrarium are foggy or if beads of water are clinging to the cover. Check to see if your terrarium needs water at least once a week although you may find that it can go six weeks at a time without any.

OPEN the lid partially at night if the walls of the terrarium are foggy. This will let the excess moisture evaporate.

FERTILIZE once a month or so with a solution about half as strong as you use on your other plants.

REMOVE any dead leaves or plants as soon as they are noticed.

KEEP the glass lid and container walls clean so that light can pass through.

REPLACE plants that begin to outgrow the terrarium or prune them back, if possible. House plants can be transplanted to pots. Woodland plants can be returned to the woods if the season allows.

ARRANGING AND DISPLAYING YOUR PLANTS

15 *Arranging and Displaying Your Plants*

There is something about having success with one plant that leads to buying others. Soon you find yourself with lots of plants and a new hobby—indoor gardening.

A single plant makes a lovely room decoration and can be placed just about anywhere. It will look well on a window sill, on or in a bookcase, on a table, on a desk, or in a tub on the floor. To display a group of plants takes a little more art. You will want to arrange your plants so that each is shown off to its full advantage while forming an attractive part of a unit.

GROUPING PLANTS

You can group plants in windows, on pebble trays, on plant stands and carts, in planters, in clusters on the floor or on furniture, or individually. Generally when you group plants, you will want your tallest ones in the back and your shortest ones forward unless the grouping is to be seen from several sides. Then you would place your tallest plant at the center and your shorter plants to the outside.

The environmental needs of your plants will determine to a large degree which plants you display together. You will group your sun-loving plants together in or near a south window and arrange shade-loving plants together in a less sunny spot. But also think of combining different leaf and plant shapes, textures, and colors to make the most attractive and interesting groupings. Under normal circumstances you won't want to put all your tall, skinny plants together on one pebble tray, for instance. They would look like a cluster of telephone poles. Nor would you want all your trailing plants together. They would make a straggly mess. A more pleasing combination would be a tall plant displayed with a medium-sized or trailing plant and a flowering plant added for color.

But there are no hard and fast rules. African violets can be displayed handsomely together just lined up on shelves. And so can cacti. And if you have a display stand that provides different levels, you can group similar plants together quite effectively. One inexpensive way to provide levels is to turn a few empty pots upside down and use them as stands for some of your plants.

A window is a natural display area. You can do all sorts of things with it. If your sill is narrow, you can buy self-attaching plant shelves that extend the sill area. Line plants up on the sill, hang a plant or two around it, train a vine up one side, and you will have a handsome window garden. Glass shelves also can be placed across the window to increase your display space and arrangement possibilities.

DISH GARDENS

A dish garden is the perfect place to group small plants with similar needs. I particularly like cactus and succulent dish gardens. All varieties of desert cactus can be grouped together in one garden. For a succulent garden, you might choose a crassula, a sansevieria, which is a tall plant with blade-like leaves, and some low-growing succulents such as sedums, echeverias, and hoyas. Dish gardens of tropical plants can be lovely, too. A small dieffenbachia would look nice with a philodendron and perhaps a dracaena or an *Aralia elegantissima.* Begonias are often displayed with English ivy.

Shallow containers like pottery bowls, clay saucers, tea cups, sherbet dishes, and even automobile hubcaps can be used for dish gardens.

Drainage is a problem in dish gardens so be sure to provide a layer of drainage material and pieces of charcoal at the bottom of your container. Cover this with a thin layer of moistened peat moss. Then add a fast-draining soil. For cacti and succulents use one of the sandy potting soils suggested in Chapter One. For other plants use one of the recommended all-purpose soils. To add interest you can place attractive rocks or pieces of driftwood in your garden.

☙ *PLANTERS*

Metal, plastic, and wooden planters are available at most garden centers. They make a convenient place to group large and medium-sized plants. Some are deep enough so that you can set your potted plants inside them. Arrange the plants in an attractive way and then surround them with moistened peat moss, perlite, vermiculite, sand, or pebbles. Be sure to provide a layer of drainage material.

If you want to plant your plants freely in the planter, provide a drainage layer of pebbles or crockery, add a little charcoal, cover with a thin layer of moistened peat moss, and then put in an inch or so of all-purpose soil. Arrange your plants and spread their roots out if you can without tearing them. Add more soil and press gently around the plants to secure them in place.

☙ *CARING FOR DISH AND PLANTER GARDENS*

Water plants in dish and planter gardens sparingly and only when soil begins to dry out. Use about half as much fertilizer for plants in these gardens as for plants in regular pots. Clean leaves monthly by sponging off with lukewarm water.

16 *Identifying Problems*

The plants discussed in this book are for the most part hardy and easy to care for, but even the best of gardeners could have problems with them.

This chart may help you discover what is wrong with a plant that is failing. A plant may have more than one problem at a time. It may be getting too much water and not enough light. Both of these problems would have to be dealt with before the plant would revive. And always be on the lookout for plant pests. They often are the cause of a plant's problem. Consult Chapter Two for directions on how to treat pest attacks.

Treat plant problems cautiously. Don't make drastic changes in a plant's environment overnight. Check out the possible causes of each symptom. Review how you have been caring for the plant. Decide what may be causing the problem and proceed with correcting the problem one step at a time. If you think improper light may be the cause, don't thrust the plant into full sun all of a sudden. Move it to brighter and brighter spots by degrees and see if the plant begins to perk up. Use moderation in dealing with your plants at all times.

Symptoms	Possible causes
No buds	Not enough light; too much or not enough plant food; temperatures too high or too low.
Leaves turn yellow	Soil doesn't drain properly; too much water; not enough plant food; too much or too little light.
Stems and leaves grow long	Not enough light; too much plant food; too much heat; not enough air circulation.
Leaf tips turn brown	Too much plant food; too much or too little water; exposure to drafts and cold air; not enough humidity; soil doesn't drain properly.
Leaves become spotted	Too much or too little water; sunburn; cold water splashed on leaves.
Leaves curl or crinkle	Too much heat; not enough humidity.
Leaves curl under	Too much light.
Lower leaves turn pale	Not enough plant food.
Leaves wilt	Too much or too little water; soil doesn't drain properly; too much heat.
Leaves turn black	Temperatures too cold, maybe freezing; sunburn; too much or too little water; not enough plant food; not enough light.
Plant doesn't grow/leaves are small	Not enough light; not enough water; not enough humidity; not enough plant food. In winter if plant seems healthy but just

	isn't growing, it may be in a period of natural dormancy.
Stem turns black/rots	Soil doesn't drain properly; too much water; plant was bruised. (Rotted parts must be cut away.)
Growth is soft in winter	Too much heat; not enough light.
White crust forms on soil or pot	Too much plant food.
Green scum forms on soil or pot	Too much plant food; soil doesn't drain properly.

Note: The size and type of pot, the consistency of the soil, and the size of the plant's root system all can determine whether a plant is getting too much or too little water. If the pot is too big for the plant, the roots will not be able to draw water out of the soil fast enough to prevent rot. If the pot is too small, the soil will not be able to retain enough moisture for the plant. If improper watering seems to be the cause of your plant's problem, always check out the pot size and the soil.

Glossary

Air-layering	A way of propagating a plant by wounding it so a portion of it will form roots and can be removed and planted. Also a way to improve the appearance of a lanky plant. (see directions on page 7)
Algae	Primitive one-celled or multi-celled plants that look like a green scum.
Bonemeal	A gentle fertilizer made of bones which have been crushed to a coarse powder.
Clay pot	The favorite pot used by horticulturalists. Made of unglazed terra-cotta.
Charcoal	A black material made of specially burned wood used as fuel and for filtering and absorbing un-

	wanted material. Charcoal suitable for indoor gardening can be bought at garden centers and pet stores. Do not use charcoal briquets for gardening.
Coarse sand	Quarried sand found at building supply stores and gardening centers. Sometimes called sharp sand. Do not use beach sand.
Crock	A broken piece of clay pot or other earthenware.
Crockery	More than one piece of broken earthenware.
Cutting	A plant part removed for the purpose of producing a new plant. Sometimes called a slip.
Dormant	Resting, not growing. (Literally, sleeping.) Many plants have periods when they grow very little or not at all. This period most often occurs in winter.
Drain	Flow through.
Drainage	The action of flowing through. Good drainage in a potted plant occurs when water flows through quickly leaving soil thoroughly moist but not soggy.
Drainage saucer	A saucer or dish that catches water from a draining pot.
Drought	A long period without rain or water.
Evaporate	To change into vapor. Water exposed to air eventually evaporates into the air—becoming water vapor.
Fertilizer	Plant food; a substance that puts nutrients into soil.
Flat	A shallow box with drainage holes in the bottom used for starting plants.
Germinate	Sprout, begin to become a plant.
Gravel	Mixture of pebbles or rock fragments.

Growing end	The tip of a stem from which new leaves form.
Humid	Containing a high amount of water vapor.
Humidity	Dampness of the air.
Humus	A substance made of partially or wholly decayed plant and animal matter. A major part of good soil; provides nutrients for plants and helps soil hold water.
Jardiniere	A large, decorative pot or stand used for plants. Small ones called cachepots.
Leaf mold	A type of humus made of decayed or decomposed leaves which have been put through a screen and sterilized.
Lukewarm	Mildly warm, tepid. (To avoid using water that is too warm, use water that feels neither warm nor cold to the touch.)
Main stem	The part of a plant to which other stems are attached. The trunk or stalk.
Mineral	A substance that is neither animal nor plant. Many minerals are found in soil and are used by plants in making food.
Mist	Spray with a fine shower of water.
Mister	Atomizer that gives off a fine spray. Used for dampening the air around plants.
Nutrient	Something that nourishes. Plants are nourished by certain minerals and gases found in air and soil. Soil nutrients get dissolved in water and are carried into the plant through roots.
Peat moss	Partially or wholly decayed plant parts from bog mosses. Used in potting soils and rooting mixtures. Helps soil hold water and gives it texture.
Pebble tray	Sided, waterproof tray which holds pebbles and

	water to a depth of at least 2 inches and is used to provide humidity to plants.
Perlite	A white gritty substance used in gardening in place of sand.
Pinch	Prune by removing young growing tips from stems and branches with scissors or fingers.
Planter	A container for holding several house plants.
Porous	Full of tiny holes or pores. Allows oxygen and water to pass through pores. Soil can be made porous with the addition of coarse sand and humus.
Pot-bound	Plant's root system has outgrown the pot. Roots have circled around and through the soil and have become matted or tightly tangled. Roots hanging out of drainage holes often are an indication that a plant is pot-bound.
Propagate	Cause to multiply. Common ways to propagate are by cuttings from plants, from seeds, by dividing a plant, by rooting an infant plant.
Prune	Cut off or pinch off plant parts for the purpose of shaping the plant or making it bushier.
Rootball	A plant's network of roots.
Seedling	The young plant that develops from a seed.
Species	A major subdivision of a plant family which shares distinctive characteristics. There can be many varieties of plants within a single species.
Sphagnum moss	Dried bog material. Used in rooting and air-layering plants.
Sprout	Begin to grow. Give off shoots or buds.
Sterile	Free from bacteria, fungus, and weeds; or, incapable of growing.
Sterilize	To make sterile.

Succulent	A type of plant with special water-storing abilities. Many can store moisture in stems and leaves for long periods making them drought-resistant.
Tight pot	A pot that cramps a plant's root system somewhat; is small in proportion to the plant's size.
Trailing plant	A plant that grows along the ground or droops over surfaces instead of growing upright.
Transpire	Give off water vapor and wastes through pores in the leaf.
Trellis	A latticework frame used to train vines.
Twist-ties	Thin pieces of paper-covered wire. Used to secure plants to supports. Also used to close plastic bags.
Vermiculite	A gritty substance made from mica and used in gardening in place of sand. Holds water.
Viable	Capable of living or germinating.
Wet feet	Term used to indicate a potted plant that is standing in water.

Bibliography

BALLARD, ERNESTA DRINKER. *Garden in Your House.* rev. enlarged ed. New York: Harper & Row, 1971.

CROCKETT, JAMES UNDERWOOD. *Flowering House Plants.* New York: Time-Life Books, 1971.

———. *Foliage House Plants.* New York: Time-Life Books, 1972.

CRUSO, THALASSA. *Making Things Grow: A Practical Guide for the Indoor Gardener.* New York: Alfred A. Knopf, 1969.

GRAF, ALFRED BYRD. *Exotic Plant Manual.* 2nd ed. East Rutherford, N.J.: Roehrs Company, 1972. This is not a general house plant guide, but an expensive and useful reference book that can be found in large libraries.

House Plants. Dell Purse Book 3858, New York: Dell Publishing Co., 1963.

JOHNSON, GEORGE V., and SMITH, FLOYD F. *Insects and Related Pests of House Plants . . . How to Control Them.* Home and Garden Bulletin No. 67, U. S. Department of Agriculture, Washington, D. C. This bulletin is available for 10¢ from The Superintendent of Documents, U. S. Printing Office, Washington, D. C.

KRAMER, JACK. *How to Grow African Violets.* Menlo Park, Cal.: A Sunset Book, Lane Books, 1972.

LANGER, RICHARD W. *The After-Dinner Gardening Book.* New York: Macmillan, 1969.

PERPER, HAZEL. *The Avocado Pit Grower's Indoor How-to Book.* New York: Walker and Company, 1965.

———. *The Citrus Seed Grower's Indoor How-to Book.* New York: Dodd, Mead, 1971.

SCHULER, STANLEY. *1001 House Plant Questions Answered.* New York: Funk & Wagnalls, 1968.

Index

V

W

Y